The Change Agent

How to Create a
Wonderful World

The Change Agent

How to Create a Wonderful World

Andrew Crofts

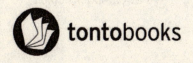

tontobooks

First published in 2010 by Tonto Books Limited

Copyright © Andrew Crofts 2010
All rights reserved

The moral rights of the author have been asserted

1

No part of this book may be reproduced or transmitted in any form or any means without written permission from the copyright holder, except by a reviewer who may quote brief passages in connection with a review for insertion in a newspaper, magazine, website, or broadcast

British Library Cataloguing in Publication Data:
A catalogue record for this book is available from the British Library

ISBN-13:
9781907183171

Printed & bound in Great Britain
by CPI Cox & Wyman

Produced up north
by Tonto Books
www.tontobooks.co.uk

To Susan, for her steadfast love and support through a variety of adventures, and to Alex, Amy, Olivia and Jess for simply being themselves.

Contents

	Introduction	ix
1	A Matter of Urgency	1
2	Arriving on the Island	13
3	Water Falls	21
4	The Future is Feminine	31
5	The Transition Generation	39
6	The Singularity	53
7	Eco-Affluence and the Happy List	63
8	The Movies	71
9	The Wide View	83
10	The Fortune Makers	93
11	Shooting Stars and Northern Lights	101
12	Sailing	109
13	Meeting the Guru	123
14	Climate Change Cities	131
15	Nuclear Sanity	143
16	Global Warming	151
17	The Bigger Picture	159
18	Refining the Human Body	167
19	The Greatest Crime Imaginable	175

Introduction

In the opening lines of his bestselling thriller *The Ghost* Robert Harris quotes me as saying:

> Of all the advantages that ghosting offers, one of the greatest must be the opportunity that you get to meet people of interest.

He then proceeds to take his ghostwriter protagonist to an island where a former prime minister is in virtual hiding. Another author's body has been washed up on the beach and an international conspiracy is unravelling.

Just as it was announced that Harris's book, which features quotes from me at the start of every chapter and with which I obviously identified strongly, was to be turned into a film I received an urgent invitation to another mysterious island.

While Roman Polanski was filming with Ewan McGregor as the writer and Pierce Brosnan as the former prime minister I was making my way to Agar's Island in Bermuda to find out what it was that was so urgent.

I was not disappointed. As the island and its owner gradually revealed their secrets I discovered that it was the very future of Homo sapiens that was at stake.

Andrew Crofts

CHAPTER ONE
A Matter of Urgency

The driver dropped us at the gates to the jetty and reversed noisily away up the steep, winding lane, leaving us alone with our suitcases. We could see the island ahead of us, but we had no idea how we were going to get there across this last stretch of water.

Even though we were only an hour or so from sunset and the night insects were already beginning to tune up, the Atlantic was still startlingly blue. The scene around us, however, had changed dramatically from the immaculate, manicured and landscaped gardens that we had been driving through since leaving the airport. All the eerily deserted, pastel-coloured mansions had vanished behind the tangle of trees and undergrowth that now surrounded us and it suddenly felt like we were the only people left in the world.

As the screech of the reversing taxi faded away, silence fell and a cool spring breeze drifted in off the shimmering water.

'What happens now?' Sue asked as we stood beside our cases.

'I'm not sure,' I admitted, gazing across at the island as if an answer would present by magic.

The rusty iron gates we had walked through looked like they hung permanently open. The stone pillars they were attached to had seemed too close for the cabbie to have wanted to risk driving through and scratching his gleaming paintwork, although there was a car safely parked up inside them under the overhanging vegetation, its wing mirrors tucked carefully in like a bird settled down for the night.

Our invitation to the island had been urgent and the flights from England hurriedly arranged. But now, in the stillness of the evening, with the waves gently lapping at the jetty beneath our feet, it felt like time had slowed to a standstill and nothing on earth could be as urgent as Jim had made it seem.

'I bought an island a few years ago,' he'd said when we met a few weeks before in Oxford. 'Extraordinary things always seem to happen there. Bring your wife with you and I'll explain everything.'

We had no idea what to expect once we had found a way to cross this final stretch of water to our destination. I hadn't heard from Jim in nearly twenty years when I saw the article in the paper announcing that he had given $100 million to Oxford University in order to create The James Martin 21st Century School, making him the biggest single donor ever to any university in Britain. He was bigger even than Sir Thomas Bodley, who donated the money for the Bodleian Library in 1598. This stands just across the road from the Old Indian Institute, which now houses Jim's 21st Century School.

I have to admit I was shocked by the size of the donation when I read the announcement. I'd known that he was doing well and was quite possibly the best in the world at what he did, but I'd had no idea just how successful he had become in the years since we had spent a week together at Tuppenny House, his beach house in Tucker's Town, an area of Bermuda we had just driven past on our way out from the airport.

The moment I read the article I was eager to find out what could have happened to generate such extraordinary wealth in the intervening years, and also to find out what Jim was hoping to achieve by making this massive investment in a futuristic school attached to the oldest university in the English-speaking world. He had been an intriguing man twenty years ago: now his story seemed to have taken on a whole new dynamic.

Jim was always a hard man to pin down because he travelled the world almost constantly, and if he wasn't travelling he would transform into a virtual recluse in order to give himself time to think and write. It was said he had written more textbooks than any other living person, some of them seminal books that had helped change the computer industry. Most of them were large books – one was almost a thousand pages. I sent out some feelers. He got back in contact surprisingly quickly to say he was about to come to England and to suggest that we should meet up because he had something urgent he needed to talk about.

'Come to the Divinity School in Oxford on March 12th,' he added. 'We're going to be making a big announcement. There'll be lots of people there you should meet. We can talk afterwards.'

Considering how huge and venerable the Divinity School is (being the oldest surviving purpose-built university building in the world), it is surprisingly hard to find if you don't know your way around the side streets and quadrangles of Oxford. Wandering back and forth past the Bodleian Library I joined forces with other lost souls on the same mission and no one we asked seemed to know quite where to direct us. By the time we eventually found someone who knew what we were looking for and entered the vaulted medieval hall, the place was already crammed with a raucous mêlée of people who obviously knew their way around the city better than I did.

Even after twenty years it was easy to spot Jim across a packed room. Taller than virtually everyone else in the crowd, despite being slightly stooped by the passing years, and immaculate in a pinstripe suit and brilliant red tie, he stood slightly separate from everyone, still obviously shy and ill at ease socially despite the fact that he must have been the focus of most of the gossip going on in the tightly knit groups of academics and journalists who filled the room around him, drinks in some hands, brochures and papers collected from the tables that lined the hall in others.

Jim wasn't engaging in conversation with anyone, nor making eye contact, just quietly and apparently contentedly waiting for the moment when he would be called upon to do whatever it was he was there for.

The university had produced a brochure called 'Oxford Thinking'. The opening sentence was a quote from John Donne: 'Change is the nursery of music, joy, life and eternity.' The centrefold contained a picture of Jim and the story of the creation of his school.

Cameras were trained on a pulpit at the far end of the room, from which announcements were obviously going to be made. It was like anticipating the curtain rising on a show and finding the stars waiting amongst the audience for their entrance cues.

Jim's obvious shyness acts like an invisible barrier around him, giving him an authority and other-worldliness that makes many nervous about approaching him, but as I weaved my way out of the crowd his face lit up with the same diffident, boyish smile I remembered from twenty years before. As I spoke he leant forward with a look of concentration, which suggested he now found it hard to hear in a room full of babbling voices, adding to the sense of distance between him and the rest of us. I noticed hearing aids in both ears and made an effort to speak louder and more clearly, hoping I didn't say anything too foolish, amplified for all around to hear, although everyone seemed too engrossed in their own conversations to be taking notice of anyone else.

'I saw an article in *The Guardian* the other day,' I ventured clumsily a few moments later to fill a conversational gap. 'It said your book was the most borrowed non-fiction title in British libraries in 2008.'

'Yes,' he nodded matter-of-factly. 'It's done well all over the world.'

'But being number one is the most incredible achievement,' I insisted, the relative popularity of different types of books being something of an obsession for me. 'That puts you in the same league as Bill Bryson and Richard Dawkins.'

I was about to add that it put him ahead of such megasellers as Sharon Osbourne, Katie Price, Russell Brand and Peter Kay as well, but decided it might take too long to explain who these people were. Would anyone in a place like this follow the gaudy world of popular culture? Would I be showing up my own appalling taste for the lowbrow in life? Or was I merely revealing an inferiority complex by even worrying about it? I was confident, anyway, that Jim would know who Bill Bryson was and I knew Richard Dawkins, most famous at that moment for his controversial book *The God Delusion*, had an involvement with Jim's 21st Century School.

'Richard was at a dinner a few months ago', Jim grinned and chuckled, 'and I asked him to say grace. He did it without a blink.'

He looked more like a mischievous schoolboy than one of the world's greatest thinkers and academic patrons, reminding me of why I had enjoyed his company so much at Tuppenny House. 'It is remarkable how successful the book has been, isn't it?'

The book in question, which so many library goers had been tempted into picking up and taking home over the previous year, was *The Meaning of the 21st Century*, a four-hundred-page 'blueprint for ensuring our future'. Hardly an easy read, despite Jim's reputation for being able to make complex subjects accessible to mere mortals and people in the street, as well as to the world leaders and corporate chieftains who had been seeking his advice for forty years or more.

The moment for the announcement of the evening was obviously approaching because the media were drawing closer to the pulpit and bustling, charming organizers appeared from the crowd to steer Jim to the right position to prepare to be introduced. He seemed entirely unperturbed by the prospect of having to stand up and speak to such an august crowd.

The Director of The 21st Century School, Ian Goldin, climbed into the pulpit first to introduce John Hood, the controversial and soon-to-be-outgoing Vice Chancellor of Oxford, who I knew had come out to the same island I was now staring at across the water when he was first appointed, in search of inspiration. He had come to hear Jim's ideas on the future and on what the greatest brains in the university should be doing about it, and had gone away with a 'to do' list that has been largely achieved during his time in power.

The Vice Chancellor came up to say a few words and then it was Jim's turn. He took to the podium with the quiet authority that has made him one of the most sought-after and well-paid speakers in the world, apparently unaware of the film cameras, and the whole room listened, straining to hear what he had to say. Jim never raises his voice – he is used to being listened to in respectful silence.

Considering that outside that hallowed hall the world was shivering its way through the most alarming financial meltdown of recent years, the announcement we had all been invited to hear was extraordinary. So convinced is Jim that the work of The 21st Century School is vital to the future of Homo sapiens that he had flown to the UK that day to announce he was willing to pledge another $50 million of his own money in 'matched funding' for the school. In other words, anything that anyone else donated to the school, up to $50 million, he would double. The scheme would end in exactly twelve months. The timing seemed preposterous. At the deepest part of the worst financial crash in living memory, when many university donors were fleeing, Jim was asking for donations on subjects related to 21st-century issues. The British are reluctant to give to universities at the best of times. The fact that he was in a position to make such as offer was a staggering achievement for a man who had earned his living for the past thirty years as a freelance writer and lecturer, having started out in a family with barely enough money to support itself.

I knew Jim had re-married since we last met, and his wife was somewhere in the room.

'Where is Lillian?' I asked when the speeches were over and Jim was standing aside from the crowd again. He pointed out a good-looking, well-groomed but unostentatious woman. She appeared to be holding court amongst a group of people in a way Jim would find difficult. I approached her and waited for a chance to introduce myself. As she talked she was moving around amongst the displays that had been set out by the fifteen (soon to be many more) institutes that were part of The 21st Century School that Jim had established. Each table was manned by enthusiastic champions aching to talk about the greatest challenges they felt faced the human species, from 'the future of the mind' to 'the future of the car', from 'nanotechnology' to 'pandemics', from 'climate change' to 'ageing', from 'oceans' to 'stem cells' ... the wealth of thinking laid out before us was dizzying.

'Lillian guards Jim fiercely,' people had warned me. 'She's his staunchest gatekeeper.'

Despite being a fully paid-up 'citizen of the world', married for many years to an Iranian before meeting Jim, who is a quintessential northern Englishman, Lillian has lost none of the Bronx accent she was brought up with as the daughter of first-generation Irish immigrants. She has a straight-talking directness, which is very different from the complicated quietness of her husband. I introduced myself nervously as soon as an appropriate moment seemed to present itself, aware that her attention was already fully occupied with the other people around her, but her response was open and reassuring, if slightly distracted.

'I hear you're coming to visit us in Bermuda,' she said.

'Yes,' I said, 'we're looking forward to it.'

I wondered if she was aware that Jim had invited me for an entire week and had suggested I bring Sue. If I were Jim's 'gatekeeper' I would probably be keen to discourage such random invasions of my privacy. One of the joys for Lillian of having a private island, after all, must be to escape from the crowds of disciples who want to sit at Jim's feet. I wondered if she had any more idea what it was Jim wanted to talk about than I did; what the urgency was all about.

She smiled sweetly but noncommittally before being whisked away again by others, leaving me pondering further about what the impending trip might bring as I moved amongst the tables and tried to absorb at least some of the information being enthusiastically expounded on all sides.

I was still pondering as I stood on the jetty with Sue and the luggage, the silent island's palm trees swaying gently in the growing wind.

There was a quiet but unbridgeable distance between Jim and his parents from the day he was born in 1933, when his mother, Mabel, nearly died of blood poisoning. For a working-class man like Tom Martin to be left with a new-born baby and a wife so sick she had to be sent away to a far-distant clinic for two years was enough to turn his hair white.

On the day his son was born Tom had backed a winning horse called Jimbo. It seemed like as good a sign as any, so he named the boy after the horse.

Tom was sporadically employed as a clerical worker in Ashby-de-la-Zouche, a small town at the very centre of England. He would not have been able to stay home on the days when he did have a job. If you didn't work in the 1930s then you would go hungry, so the baby was handed around amongst any female friends and relatives in the community who were willing and able to take a turn at childcare.

Jim later found out that the clinic his mother was in, in the southern seaside resort of Hastings, was extremely expensive, but he never discovered who paid the fees. Such delicate matters would never be discussed in the coming years.

When Mabel was eventually discharged from the clinic and arrived home she was still paralyzed down one side of her body and seemed to have fallen into a resigned silence with life. She and Tom came from a time and a class that was used to stoicism and 'getting by'. It can't have been long, however, before they must have realized their little son was going to be different from the rest of the family.

Lillian recently came across Jim's early kindergarten reports in which a teacher wrote of 'fits of nursery naughtiness' and 'lapses of moral vertigo that inevitably end in disasters'.

Jim has no memories of what those fits and lapses might have consisted of, or indeed what 'moral vertigo' might be, but he does remember that they resulted in him being expelled from the kindergarten at one stage, with a recommendation to his surprised parents that they should 'consult a psychologist' with the boy.

Tom was outraged by such a suggestion, but Mabel took Jim to see the doctor anyway, who agreed with Tom that there was nothing wrong with their son that a stern telling off wouldn't put right.

As the years passed, the distance between Jim and his parents never narrowed. To a practical man like Tom, his son undoubtedly seemed like a hopeless dreamer, and it is possible that he felt intimidated by the obvious and burgeoning intelligence the awkward little boy was starting to display.

Despite the fact that his father seemed to be permanently irritated by his existence, although Jim could never work out what it was that he was doing wrong, he was perfectly contented and self-contained through his childhood. Although his parents left him pretty much to his own devices there were some domestic chores that had to be done as soon as he was big enough.

Every day, regardless of the weather, he had to take two buckets out into the fields and collect sheep's droppings. He had to fill the buckets, bring them home and dump the droppings into a water butt. This produced a liquid fertilizer for feeding the vegetables and flowers that Tom grew for their own consumption and for bartering with neighbours in exchange for freshly caught game or fish. Wartime rationing meant that everything was in short supply and Jim was introduced early to the idea of using his ingenuity to make the most of what was available, scavenging happily in the hedgerows and woods for berries and mushrooms when the seasons were right.

Wandering in the fields with his buckets, his eyes half on the ground in search of droppings to be saved and half on the surrounding scenery, his mind was already beginning to puzzle over questions that he would not have been able to voice over the family tea table without risking a sharp clip round the ear for 'trying to be smart'. In his daydreams he fantasized that his parents were merely charged with looking after him until he was ready to go out into the world.

The Martin family had lived in the same little market town for as long as anyone could remember – presumably for centuries. Its boundaries circumscribed the world that Tom and Mabel were comfortable in, and although it was a perfectly pleasant place to live, it wasn't long before Jim's *imagination began to long for wider horizons. Their tiny house overlooked the local castle, which had been destroyed by Cromwell and was made the setting for* Ivanhoe *by Sir Walter Scott. It had a high keep (tower) and was reputed to have the second-largest kitchen in England, after Windsor Castle's. As soon as he was old enough to go on adventures on his own Jim would scramble up the side of the keep, wriggle in through a window and climb a staircase to the top. The castle gave him his first glimpse of the possibilities of life beyond the restrictions of school and the Martin family home.*

CHAPTER TWO
Arriving on the Island

As I gazed across the water, wondering what to do next, there was a sudden whirl of activity around my legs, making me jump back in surprise. A light-footed fox terrier was dancing around in a frenzy of excitement, his lips curled up above his teeth in a gesture that I guessed was meant to be an excited smile but came off looking more like a snarl.

'Tucker! Here boy!'

I turned to see the dog's master emerging from between two small, weather-beaten cottages that I had hardly noticed amongst the undergrowth at the side of the jetty, my attention having been taken up with the departing taxi driver and the island ahead. I saw that the cottage nearest to the water had been painted almost the same postcard blue as the sea, and there was another paler one nestled behind it. Now that I was focusing on them I could see that around them in the shadows of the trees were makeshift pergolas crowded with hanging baskets, which looked as if they had been planted up to be sold rather than to be displayed where they hung. Below them were plants and pots of all descriptions and sizes and it was from the midst of all this verdant chaos that the gangling form of Tucker's master was emerging, his hand outstretched in greeting, his face creased with many years of sunshine, long grey hair pulled tightly back in a ponytail and a broad smile beaming through a straggling grey beard.

'Hi,' he said. 'I'm Paul. I've rung over to tell them you're here.' Shakespeare had heard tales of the newly discovered island of Bermuda, or 'Devil's Island' as the sailors of the time had named it, and used the descriptions that he heard while writing his final play, *The Tempest*. Paul could have stepped straight out of Shakespeare's imagination four hundred years ago, as could much of the scene around us.

'How lush and lusty the grass looks!' Shakespeare's Gonzalo said of the island. 'How green! ... Here is everything advantageous to life.'

'How do you come to be living here?' I asked Paul as we waited together for something to happen on the other side of the water. I wanted to know everything about his life but had other things on my mind at that moment.

'It's a long story,' he grinned. 'I came from Kent in England originally. I work in the gardens on the island for Dr Martin.'

To me there always seems to be something romantic about people who have travelled great distances and have decided to settle on tiny islands, particularly if they look like hermits and completely unlike most of their fellow islanders.

'So we'll be bumping into you over there during our stay?' I said.

'More than likely.'

Later I would hear Paul describe his tumbledown cottage as 'the hobbit-hole' and he could indeed have been a character emerging from Middle Earth to greet us just as easily as a character from the stage of Shakespeare's Globe.

It was as if the sudden noise of Tucker appearing at our ankles had woken the sleeping island and there were flurried signs of life on the jetty as two figures emerged from the dock house, jumped into a motorized skiff and headed across the two or three hundred meters of water to the small clearing where we were waiting. As they drew closer I could see that the taller of the two figures was Jim, waving with all the guileless enthusiasm of a boy on a *Swallows and Amazons* adventure. There are moments when it is still easy to imagine the young child wandering around the fields with his buckets nearly seventy years ago, picking up sheep's droppings to feed his father's garden.

His companion, a smaller, wirier man, was operating the boat. Jim had mentioned there was an 'island manager' who lived there more or less permanently while he and Lillian travelled around the world researching and lecturing, but I had already discovered there was much more history to the relationship than that description suggested. Not only was Duncan managing the island, he was also its co-creator, the architect of the extraordinary house that now towered up out of the palm trees, and of the many ponds and gardens stretching down the steep slopes to the bays and inlets around the island's coastline.

'It has been said', Jim later joked lugubriously, 'that if Duncan was Michelangelo, I was the Pope.'

The two men had been friends since the days of Tuppenny House, when they had met as neighbours. Duncan had provided some of the illustrations for *Technology's Crucible*, a book that Jim wrote in the 1980s, in which he accurately predicted many of the technological developments that occurred over the next twenty years, setting the story in a Utopia that I could easily imagine had now come to pass for real here on Agar's Island.

Duncan had been one of the first to land on the island with Jim, hacking through the tangled undergrowth with a machete as they tried to work out how to make such an abandoned wilderness habitable, never realizing at the time that it would become a ten-year project and was still not entirely finished. I felt a frisson of excitement as the skiff drew closer to the jetty.

As they pulled up Tucker entered a rising cycle of hysteria at so much unexpected activity enlivening his evening, whirling like a dervish on his hind legs in a state of ecstatic joy. Our cases were passed down from the jetty and we set off, leaving Paul and Tucker to return for the night to the seclusion and tranquillity of their hobbit-hole.

During the long and fraught reconstruction of the island rumours had abounded in Bermuda as to the identity of the mysterious owner and what his plans might be for this latest hideaway. Tourist boats would circle it on their regular beat between the city of Hamilton and the dockyards where the largest cruise liners would moor when they were unable to get any closer to the pretty pastel-coloured waterfront of the capital, and the guides would weave tales over megaphones, which could often be heard from the island if the wind was in the right direction to carry them.

At one stage the delivery of a pair of giant stone lions from China grew into a story that a selection of live big cats were being imported on to the island by a Japanese billionaire, and that the Bermudian government was demanding they be removed immediately to somewhere more suitable, 'such as Puerto Rico'.

Other stories told of wild parties held in underground rooms and of battles with the government's planning authorities to allow the construction of the eccentric, eclectic building that Duncan and Jim had imagined together as they gradually tamed the island and grew familiar with its hidden treasures.

'The island is haunted by the ghosts of nineteenth-century convicts.'

'The island used to be an aquarium and the new owner has converted it into a harem with a different girl in each of the glass tanks.'

In fact there actually had been an aquarium, opened on New Year's Day in 1908 by possibly the greatest of all-American writers, Mark Twain. But it had proved to be a fiasco and was closed down. Watching the tangled island draw closer it wasn't hard to imagine Huckleberry Finn or

Tom Sawyer sitting fishing on one of the little jetties, or padding barefoot amongst the densely planted trees.

We reached the island's main jetty in a matter of minutes. Two apricot-coloured 'labradoodles' were pacing excitedly back and forth in front of the dock house, taking over guard duties from Tucker on the other side of the water. Our arrival and the business of getting our cases on to the battered-looking solar-powered golf cart caused a momentary flutter of activity in the usually quiet moments before sunset. The scents of jasmine and pittosporum trees filled the air as Duncan and one of the dogs took the cart up to the house and we followed at a gentle pace on foot.

Jim was twinkling with pride as we looked around us in awe, passing under long walks of pergolas covered in roses and bougainvillea and past entrances to hidden quarry gardens, one of them guarded by the towering stone lions who were the cause of the tourist boat rumours.

'They were outside a hotel where I was staying in Guilin in China,' Jim explained as we paused to look up at them. 'I said how much I admired them and how great they would look on the island without realizing that my hosts would then feel honour bound to give them to me. But when the Chinese shipping company got out their maps they could find no sign of Bermuda anywhere. It was too insignificant a speck in the ocean for anyone to have added it. They insisted that the islands must therefore not exist and the lions had to be sent to New York and shipped on from there. The container weighed thirty tons. We had a crane on the island at the time but the weight was too much and made it topple over with the first lion it lifted.'

The lions survived the crash and a forest of bamboo had grown up in the quarry behind them, with the towers of the house we were heading for peeking out from above the jungle that had risen to soften the lines of the building and quieten the fears of the Bermudian authorities who were nervous that the structure would appear stark and out of character amongst the other islands. In fact, despite its extraordinary height, the house looks like it has been there forever, becoming almost an organic part of the foliage surrounding it.

'I liked the idea of living on an island because of the isolation,' Jim said. 'It provides time and quietness for thinking, for clarity. I didn't want to create an English garden with flowerbeds that need weeding and lawns that need mowing, I wanted it to be natural but full of exotic flowering plants and meandering paths that would be nice for walking on. But of course at the beginning I had no idea of what was hiding beneath the rocks.'

We continued the steep climb up through the greenery, past carpets of blue bermudiana interspersed with wild orange gladioli, to the front of the house where Lillian and Duncan were waiting by the golf cart to welcome us officially.

🌐

On November 14th 1940 a seven-year-old Jim stood at his parents' bedroom window gazing out at a column of flame and smoke that reached miles into the night sky, the cloud spreading horizontally and blocking out the light of the moon. He was partly excited by the drama of the spectacle he was witnessing and partly lost in thought as he tried to work out what it could all mean.

The industrial city of Coventry, twenty miles from where he was standing, was burning. Five hundred German bombers, wave after wave, were dropping five hundred tons of high explosives and one hundred and fifty thousand incendiary bombs on to the city centre and industrial targets around the outskirts. The Rolls Royce factory in Derby, some miles away, escaped, being surrounded by barrage balloons filled with hydrogen to make it too dangerous for the planes to fly over.

The fire continued to rage for two more days and apart from causing many hundreds of deaths the bombs also destroyed more than sixty thousand buildings, including the most magnificent fourteenth-century cathedral in the country. The photographs of Coventry after the attack looked like Berlin in 1945.

Sometimes during those war years stray bombs would fall on Ashby-de-la-Zouche too, particularly on the nearby railway lines that carried steam trains. Lying in bed on wet days, Jim could hear sudden irregular bursts of puffing as their wheels skidded on the incline. At weekends Tom would take his lad to view the damage and even today, nearly seventy years later, he can still remember the smell of earth and tar in the local air raid shelter where they would sometimes go to seek safety when the bombers were on their way.

Tom had been in the army himself and when he was out drinking at the British Legion with his friends they would exchange stories about the idiocies of the officers who had been put in charge of them. Sometimes Tom seemed unaccountably irritated by the whole world, especially by his day-dreaming son.

Jim listened quietly to everything the grown-ups talked about, unsure what to make of the things he was seeing and hearing, trying to find the sense of it all, struggling to see some sort of pattern that might predict how these appalling events and dramatic scenes of apparent madness and pointless destruction going on around him might affect his life in the future. He didn't feel particularly afraid, more puzzled and eager to find answers to the questions he no longer dared to voice around the tea table for fear of provoking his father's impatience.

CHAPTER THREE
Water Falls

It's always an awkward few minutes when you first arrive as someone's house guest before you all find a comfortable level for co-habiting. You want to praise something about the home in order to show your gratitude for their hospitality, but you don't want to sound ridiculously effusive. At the same time as wanting to show off their house, the hosts want to insist that you make yourself comfortable and assure you that they want you to feel that you can treat their home as your own, while many years of social conditioning tell you it would be inappropriate to interpret that request too literally too soon, but at the same time you want to be as light a burden on them as possible by looking after your own needs wherever you can ... It inevitably takes a while to settle into a routine with which everyone feels comfortable.

Lillian must be more than usually well practiced at welcoming a variety of strangers into her home. She was waiting for us at the top of the hill beside Duncan and the parked golf cart beneath the glass walls of an atrium, which rose twenty-four feet out of the shadows of the palm trees and into the reddening sky. Unloading our cases, we followed her into the house.

How do you stop yourself from exclaiming in amazement when every corner you turn you enter yet another extraordinary room filled with artefacts and design ideas from other parts of the world? Behind the mighty, vine-draped atrium that is the face the house shows most often to the outside world, our host and hostess led us through a reception hall of the darkest, shiniest African wood out into the brightness of a quadrangle that could have come from a north African medina or a small Spanish town in a spaghetti western. A giant Chinese bell hung in a bell tower on the far side of the quadrangle, above a mighty pair of wooden doors, and water flowed through mosaic-lined ponds and fountains past an ancient pittosporum tree, which had been the original inspiration for the design and construction of the beds and seats and paths that surrounded it.

The towering, glassed-in arches along one side of the quadrangle led past a library and cinema room up a sweeping stone staircase to the kitchen wing, while staircases on the other side led to bedrooms on any number of different floors and levels, every door opening up to reveal views of sparkling waters, passing boats and the distant mainland of Bermuda itself on the other side of the bay.

Used to travelling constantly, Jim and Lillian knew exactly how long to allow us to be alone in our room to acclimatize ourselves to our new surroundings before suggesting we met outside for drinks before supper.

Half an hour later we were sitting in a three-hundred-year-old Balinese wooden temple, which Jim informed us had arrived on the island via Africa in a hundred separately wrapped and numbered pieces, like a three-dimensional jigsaw puzzle. It now stands on its own island in the centre of a pond full of huge koi carp. We sipped wine as our jangled travellers' nerves were soothed by the sound of water cascading down the walls of the former quarry that were sheltering us from the growing wind. There was an obvious closeness between Jim and Lillian, visible in the way their eyes met as they talked.

There's no source of fresh water on Bermuda apart from what falls from the sky, so every house is required by law to have a clean white roof that captures the rain and channels it to darkened underground tanks for later use. On Agar's Island the capture and recycling of rain water has been turned into a precise science.

Part of the reason why the island had become little more than a rock covered in dense scrub was because any good earth that might have managed to accumulate over the centuries was constantly being washed away into the sea by the rains whenever they struck. One of the first tasks facing Jim and Duncan had been to direct every drop of water into a variety of tanks: one for drinking water, one for general household water, one for lavatories and other waste, and one for irrigating the garden, all of them controlled by computers.

Once the system was up and running it was then possible to build a series of water gardens and ponds fed by waterfalls and carefully guided streams, keeping it moving and refreshed.

'Water is one of the biggest problems on the planet,' Jim said, tossing a handful of fish food in amongst the circling carp, enticing them to rear up out of the water in a shimmering, shivery scrum of white, black and golden fins and scales. 'More people in the developing world die from drinking bad water than die of Aids, yet it could easily be sorted out. If you go to some of the most water-stressed places on the planet you'll see no gutters or water butts. During the monsoon seasons the rain all runs into the streets, often mixing with sewage and dead rats so that it becomes not only unusable but actually life threatening. Then the droughts come and there is no water stored to keep the crops or livestock alive and the women have to walk miles to wells to collect putrid water, which has to be boiled before it is even drinkable.

'Without water there is soon no plant life and no foliage and without foliage that will fall and rot with the passing seasons there will eventually be no fertile soil to support human and animal life. A lack of water will cause wars because people will be fighting for their very survival. It would be the simplest thing in the world to build tanks to catch rain water and to teach people how to keep it clean. We're using up most of our water resources, the ones that have been stored up in underground aquifers for thousands of years, so very soon a large part of the world will be completely relying on what comes out of the sky, just like we are here.

'When Bermudians travel they are amazed at the waste of water they see everywhere – houses with roofs that don't catch rain and property that allows all the rain water to run away. Most of the world's rain soaks uselessly into the ground. The use of drip irrigation can increase the yield of most crops up to four times.'

Jim deliberately tossed some of the food on to a ledge of rocks at the edge of the water. The fish were so eager to snap up whatever was given to them, despite the fact the pond water around them was thick with natural foods that they could graze on to their hearts' content, that they fought and wriggled their way clear out of the water, twisting and flapping desperately on the rock shelf in order to get back to the life-supporting water once they had devoured every last scrap within reach.

Jim chuckled. 'Just like investment bankers – willing to risk life itself for a few extra mouthfuls that they don't even need.'

He gestured to the cool, watery scene around us, the lilies on the surface above the carp, the vines trailing down through the waterfalls and the thick, flower-speckled tropical growth all round the edges.

'Ten years ago all this water would have disappeared into the sea with only the toughest and least useful of plant life left clinging to the rocks. We are using ancient peasant farming methods, just like my father growing vegetables with sheep manure. The sun, wind and water are all there for us, we simply have to capture and harness them. If only all of the problems facing us had such potentially simple solutions.

'People cannot live without enough water because they can't grow food. There isn't enough for us to allow it to just drain away. We have to learn to husband our resources and use them productively. Every year humanity loses a hundred million acres of farmland and twenty-four billion tons of topsoil, and we create fifteen million acres of new desert around the world. An inch of good topsoil can take a thousand years to form but when we cut down trees and destroy windbreaks it can be washed or blown away in months. We speeded up the restoration of the soil here by asking friends with horses and cows to let us have their manure. We brought it over on barges and that gave us enough topsoil to start planting, which gave nature the opportunity it needed to get the circle of life re-started.'

We all fell silent for a moment, sipping our wine, listening to the night songs of the toads and insects around us, watching the beautiful, stupid fish battling for the last of the treats that had fallen on them so unexpectedly from the sky.

'Nature does come back if you give it a chance,' Jim said. 'If you go down to South Africa you'll see that the whales are returning now and their numbers will soon be back to where they were before we started killing them. We're going to know a lot more about the oceans in the coming years through developments in technology and even though we have destroyed ninety per cent of the edible fish in the oceans we'll be able to rebuild the stocks that we've exhausted. It'll be a slow process for the first few years while we wait for the new stocks to reach breeding ages, but once you've passed that point the process can become very fast.

'We're already making computer models of entire oceans and soon we'll be able to do it far better. With global positioning systems on every boat we will be able to know exactly where they are at every moment and at the same time we will be using them to be constantly collecting information. The planet will soon be covered with instrumentation and computers studying and learning the minutiae of how it works and how it can be saved. It's the same with reclaiming the forests. There is so much technological development happening but we have to know how to use it wisely.'

It was so pleasant sitting in the fading light on an island thousands of miles from whatever else might have been preying on my mind at home. I quite forgot that Jim had summoned me as a matter of urgency. I always found him the easiest and most soothing of company. Sue sometimes accuses me of being 'a human hoover', firing endless streams of questions at anyone who has the bad luck to find him or herself trapped beside me at a dinner party or in any other social situation. I'm always more comfortable being on the asking end of a conversation rather than the answering.

'People sometimes find it intimidating,' she tells me, and I do my best to ration my thirst for information in order to remain within appropriate social guidelines, but my curiosity generally gets the better of me.

With Jim there is no such problem. The man's head is stuffed to bursting with more than half a century of research, experience, reading and thinking. He never seems to tire of answering questions, of explaining or trying to enlighten on any subject that he feels he can help with. He never makes me feel like I'm asking stupid questions, or impertinent or prying ones. It's like sinking your head into a warm, comforting bath of wisdom.

Tom Martin might not have known what to make of his shy, awkward only child, but Mr Woodcock, the headmaster of Ashby-de-la-Zouche Grammar School did. The headmaster (known inevitably as 'Timber Dick' by the pupils) was a fierce and effective believer in searching out the brightest children with the most potential and developing them for places at Oxford and Cambridge, where their minds could really be let loose and allowed to fly. He was particularly keen on directing them towards Oxford, his own alma mater.

Mr Woodcock very quickly spotted the academic potential of the strange, enthusiastic and endlessly curious young Jim Martin.

It was the sciences that Jim was going to be specializing in, particularly physics, but his curiosity and interests led him in every direction right from the start. Overcoming his shyness, he did some acting, playing Bottom in A Midsummer Night's Dream, *which was his first introduction to Shakespeare and to a world of theatre and literature that Tom and Mabel and the rest of his family couldn't help him with. Tom and his drinking mates were actively suspicious of anything that smacked of pretension and Shakespeare certainly fell an uncomfortable distance inside the borders of that category.*

At a practical level Jim also enjoyed inventing and building things, creating a bicycle with just one pedal so his mother could ride around town despite the fact that she was still partially paralyzed down one side of her body. Delighted by her renewed mobility, Mabel chose to ignore the loud clunking sound that her inventor son seemed to be unable to overcome in his contraption. He also built a speedometer for his own bike, and a mechanical contraption for playing noughts and crosses, and a machine for drawing patterns using the turntable of an old phonograph. If computers had been invented at that stage he would undoubtedly have been a child hacker.

Jim has a theory that only-children can be more self-sufficient than those with siblings, and that they sometimes dare to think different thoughts, perhaps because there are fewer people around to bring them back to earth and puncture their dreams. He thinks that as a result of having more time alone in their own heads they can end up being creative and different from others.

Happy to spend a fair amount of time on his own, he developed an interest in astronomy, building telescopes from old lenses he had persuaded the local optician to give him, the barrels made from cardboard tubes. The results were powerful enough to allow him to view the four moons of Jupiter.

By scrounging a variety of chemicals he learned to dissolve phosphorous in carbon disulphide and produced a liquid which, when poured on to the concrete of the back yard, caused it to glow eerily in the dark, but also caused his trousers to spontaneously combust after a spillage.

Tom was close to despair over the antics of this strange, other-worldly boy who didn't seem to fit in with any of the established certainties of masculine life in a small town. Nothing he could do could persuade Jim to show the slightest interest in sport and other traditionally manly activities, and the boy seemed to be reading the oddest of books whenever he wasn't causing mischief. He would be reading about cybernetics one week and Galileo the next.

One author who had caught Jim's attention was Fred Hoyle, an inventive astronomer who had written titles such as The Nature of the Universe. One day, when Jim heard that Hoyle was coming to lecture scientists at the nearby Rolls Royce plant, he persuaded a friend to smuggle him in and sat spellbound as the great man filled the blackboard with mathematics that Jim couldn't yet hope to understand but which made him all the more determined to learn.

The calculations appeared to prove conclusively that it was impossible for humans ever to build a chemically powered rocket that would orbit the earth. Six years later the Russians launched Sputnik and Jim went back to Hoyle's workings to try to understand how so great a thinker could have been so wrong. He realized that although the calculations had been correct they had only applied to a single-stage rocket. A failure of imagination had meant that Hoyle had not considered the prospect of building a multi-stage rocket.

Jim saw at that moment that to achieve really groundbreaking leaps forward you needed to be able to combine imagination with scientific discoveries. He read that Arthur C Clarke had said *'Nearly everything is possible if you just look for the right way to do it.'* He couldn't wait to find out more, to become more educated, to understand the universe better, and to find out what the 'right way' might be.

Becoming fascinated with computers and the changes they might make to the world, Jim organized a meeting at his school's Scientific Society to describe IBM's 701 computer and to explain how much faster he believed machines would become in the future. The Senior Science Master, who had never heard of the IBM 701, was not impressed.

'The Scientific Society', he told Jim sternly, 'is a respectable society. There must never be another meeting like this. This not an "American" science club.'

For Tom and Mabel the prospect of leaving even Ashby-de-la-Zouche was unthinkable, let alone entering a world as foreign and rarefied as Oxford, filled, as Tom was certain it would be, with the sort of foolish sons of rich men he had encountered as officers in the army. How, he wondered, did the headmaster think he was going to be able to afford to send his son to such a place when he could barely make enough to feed and clothe his small family?

Jim knew what a struggle life was for his father during the depression years, having come across the normally proud and emotionless man crying like a bereft child after losing yet another job and having no idea how he was going to earn enough to support his wife and son. Even when the headmaster explained that he intended to coach Jim for a scholarship and that the education would cost the family nothing, Tom was still wary. He wished he could think of a proper job that his son could do in their home town without the need for a fancy education.

'Why don't you become a mailman?' he asked Jim when he could think of nothing else to suggest.

Funnily enough, in the month when I arrived at Agar's Island, the production company Merchant Ivory was preparing to release a film in which the opening scenes would see Jim acting the part of a mailman, but that was certainly not what Tom had in mind at the time he suggested it.

CHAPTER FOUR
The Future is Feminine

As Jim and I brought the glasses and empty bottle back up to house I noticed a picture of an adult Corinthia standing amongst a collection of childhood photographs. Even though I hadn't seen her since she was fourteen and I was staying with them at Tuppenny House, I immediately knew it was her, and I guessed that Jim was the photographer. Two of the great loves of his life were his only daughter from his first marriage and the art of photography.

When I first met Corinthia her mother had recently died and she and Jim were adjusting to living together. He was a man who was not used to dealing with children, and probably hadn't been very good at it even when he was a child himself, while she was a child who had just lost the most important person in her life. They also had a permanent nanny living in the house, who had become pretty much a surrogate mother to Corinthia during those difficult years.

At the time Corinthia had been about to go off to boarding school in Canada and even by then it was easy to see that she was growing into a beautiful woman. The photograph on the side, which was probably taken when she was in her twenties, looked like the cover of a glossy magazine, with Corinthia's skilfully made-up face looking out from a background of lush, dark foliage, suggesting it had been taken in some exotic location.

'What's Corinthia doing now?' I asked, picking the frame up to take a closer look.

'She's an architect in Washington,' Jim replied. 'Doing well with her career but finding it hard to find the right sort of man.'

'So no grandchildren yet?'

'No. Lillian has four children and none of them have produced any grandchildren for us yet either.' He paused for a second before developing that particular thread of thought. 'It's a trend that may, of course, save the human race.'

With Jim virtually all small talk leads immediately back to the big subjects, the ones that obsess him and have done for years: mainly the future of the human race and the planet that we inhabit.

'How do you mean?' I asked, carefully replacing the photograph amongst the others.

'Educating women is one of the fundamental keys to making the transition into a spectacular new phase of human evolution. I've spent a great deal of time working and filming in some of the worst shanty cities in the world. If the population continues to climb at the current rate, and if climate change also continues to put pressure on the poorer areas of the world, the situation is going to become far, far worse. Millions of people are living in conditions that are worse than anything that was happening four or five hundred years ago, and they are multiplying at a terrible rate, constantly making the situation worse and putting more pressure on the world's resources, particularly in their own local areas. If we are going to avert catastrophe it's crucial that women take more control of their own lives and bodies.

'A woman with no education at all in a poor country will have an average of six to eight children. If she is taught to read that number will drop to around three. If she is able to hold down a decent job and earn money, then the number drops again, perhaps to two. When you get to a level where women can actually compete for the most interesting careers,' he gestured towards Corinthia's picture, 'outnumbering the boys in establishments like medical schools and law schools, then they tend to get married later and put off having babies, and the birth rate drops yet again. Women don't want to give up their good salaries. In Taiwan, where women have jobs like business managers and investment bankers, the average is point seven children per woman. It has dropped from about seven to point seven, and women have interesting lives. The way to bring the world's population back down to a sustainable level is to educate women like men. You can give women better lives and solve one of the world's biggest problems at the same time.'

'Is it realistic to think you can do that in time?' I asked as we went back through to the kitchen.

'It is realistic that we could make a start on ensuring that every girl is taught to read, and is taught to understand that she can have some say over what happens to her own body and her own womb; to convince her that she doesn't have to have a child every year just because her partner refuses to use contraceptives. The problem is that in some cultures the men are allowed to use physical force to dominate and rape their women. If they refuse to use contraceptives there is little the women can do to protest unless they want to risk a beating. In many of the shanty cities there are no family units. The women mostly bring up the children on their own and often they find themselves in the situation purely through ignorance and lack of education.

'But this is only one of the changes that has to happen. For Homo sapiens to survive this century we have to accept that almost everything is going to have to change.'

He looked very serious and said, 'We need change agents who understand the big changes that are possible.'

Supper was laid out on the kitchen table, which was another dizzying invention from Duncan and Jim: a circular table hanging from the ceiling on reinforced steel wires, swaying gently at every touch. It hung above a circular glass floor. Looking down through the floor I could see a stone shaft about nine feet in diameter plunging down twenty feet to a mosaic of glass at the bottom, like a well without water. We sat on see-through, swivel Perspex chairs, suspended above the shaft much as the table was suspended above our knees. Nothing, it seemed, was quite as you would expect on this island.

'When we came across this shaft during our excavations', Jim said, following my gaze down to the gaping hole beneath our feet, 'it was full of debris. At the top we found stuff from the 1950s like old-fashioned OXO bottles, but the further down we dug the more ancient the rubbish was, until eventually we started to bring up things from the time of Dickens, like the sort of clay pipes you see men smoking in Victorian illustrations. We eventually discovered that it was an old limekiln built by the first settlers on Bermuda, with a tunnel at the base for stoking the fire.'

The roots of this house, it seemed, bore down deep into the rocks and history below.

'Think of the twenty-first century as a deep river canyon with a narrow bottleneck at its centre.' Jim returned to his previous train of thought. 'Imagine humanity as a raft plunging downstream at an unstoppable speed. As we head into the canyon we'll have to cope with a rate of change that becomes much more intense, like a white-water raft trip with the currents becoming infinitely faster and rougher, a time when technology will accelerate at a phenomenal rate.'

Jim was using bottles and glasses to construct a model of the river and the raft that he could see in his mind's eye in order to demonstrate more vividly exactly what was going to happen, like a boy with a new train set.

'At this narrow part of the canyon, the world's population will be at its highest and the world's resources will be under their greatest stress. But the decades in which we are being swept towards the canyon bottleneck will be a time when we will unlock extraordinary new technology: nanotechnology, biotechnology, extreme-bandwidth networks, robotic factories, regenerative medicine and intense forms of computerized intelligence. Huge leaps forward will be made and the damage done by our abuse of nature could slowly start to be corrected. Educating women to take a more proactive role in developing countries, as they already are doing in developed countries, is just one of the fundamental changes we need to get through the canyon.'

The arrival of his first bicycle when he was around ten was the first of many events that would lead to Jim's world opening up in a quantum leap. Tom and Mabel were happy for him to pedal off for as many hours as he wanted as long as he wasn't meant to be at school or doing chores around the house or garden. Suddenly he was no longer restricted to visiting the places he could reach on foot. In the company of other like-minded boys he would set off exploring new horizons in a pattern that would gradually develop over the coming decades until his wanderings embraced the entire globe.

In the 1940s England was still full of stately country houses built on the proceeds of the Industrial Revolution that the owners could no longer afford to keep going, many of which had been used to billet soldiers during the war. Some were just locked up and left to rot, no doubt in the hope that good times would eventually return so that the dust sheets could be removed and the leaking roofs repaired. Many, however, were scheduled for demolition, their often elegant detailing lost forever.

Jim and his gang of fellow cyclists discovered that it was often not hard to find a loose shutter or a tradesman's entrance that had been overlooked by whoever had secured the buildings and would allow them to wriggle inside and view the wonders of another world. They would go from room to room, throwing open double doors and climbing grand, sweeping staircases, their eyes wide with amazement at the sights they were seeing.

In one house they came across a silver bathtub with a hood containing jets and nozzles to spray the bather from every angle, which Jim later discovered had been installed to ensure King Edward VII would be comfortable when he came to stay. Not only was the tub solid silver, but so were the hood and nozzles. At the time he knew nothing about the history of the piece, merely marvelling at the dozens of spouts designed to bring hot water to every part of His Majesty's body, intrigued by the ingenuity of the engineering and wondering what it would feel like to live in a world full of such luxuries.

The same house had a magnificent chapel containing a large pipe organ, and a music room where Handel had written the Messiah, *with brocade-like crimson wallpaper flaking off the walls.*

What struck Jim most strongly as he wandered around the rooms of these great places was how different the scale was to the little houses he and his friends were used to. The taller he grew physically, and the broader his knowledge of the outside world became, the more cramped he felt in his childhood home. He could easily imagine how wonderful it would be to be surrounded by so much space and light and such beautiful works of art every hour of the day, but he couldn't imagine how anyone got to be in a position to be able to afford to enjoy such wonders. He had seen all too clearly how hard his father had to struggle simply to keep them off the breadline: how did a person go from merely surviving like Tom to owning and running all this?

In one house the boys managed to make their way up a dusty wooden staircase to the lead-covered roof, where the summer sun was beating down, providing them with natural sunbeds to lie and daydream on with their shirts off, soaking up the rays and the warmth of the heavy lead beneath them. As the others messed about around him Jim was viewing the grounds below, dotted with peacefully grazing sheep, able to see the way in which past owners had designed and ordered the landscapes around their home. He realized that little of the beautiful scenery they had cycled through was actually as nature had created it and it thrilled him to think that mere humans could create and control something so massive and sweeping as the parklands that stretched out around them.

He thought of the way in which Tom designed and ordered his flowerbeds and vegetables and imagined how it would feel to be able to do the same over thousands of acres of your own land, creating vistas of trees and lakes as far as the eye could see from every window of your home.

What impressed him the most was that the people who had actually designed and built the sweeping landscapes had been thinking of what these views would look like in the future, many years after they themselves would be dead. For a landscape and its varied trees to mature to the full beauty of the designer's imagination might take a century or even two. He was excited by the thought of being able to make a difference to the world for future generations.

The possibilities of life quickened his heart as he thought about them, but at the same time the logistics of how to achieve such a position puzzled him. He was already aware that his best chance of ever being able to inhabit and create worlds like these was to allow his headmaster to guide him on the mysterious path to being the sort of man who could move landscapes, gaze on wonderful views whenever he chose and live amongst beautiful things. If he became a mailman, as Tom was suggesting, he would never get closer than peering through the letterboxes of houses like these.

In the coming years many of the stately homes that Jim and his friends had infiltrated would be demolished, almost as if someone was trying to erase all evidence of that prewar generation of wealth and superiority, but in many cases the gardens and landscapes around the vanished buildings lived on and continued to evolve, and the seeds they had sown in Jim's young imagination were taking root.

Once he had discovered the freedom that his bicycle offered him, Jim was constantly pushing the boundaries of his world further and further away from Ashby-de-la-Zouche. He discovered that it was actually possible to cycle to London within a few hours, particularly if he could manoeuvre the bike into the slipstream of a lorry so that it would be pulled along at thirty or forty miles an hour with virtually no effort required on his behalf. The buzz of the streets in the capital city, and the splendour of the architecture, even after the damage wrought by the German bombs, made him eager to travel further and to learn and see more.

It was a revelation to find that he could go wherever he wanted and it didn't have to cost money as long as he was willing to sleep in barns and ditches along the way, drink water and eat bread and cheese. He was more than willing to put up with physical discomforts if it meant he could explore. Having got to London it was not long before he found ways to get across the Channel to Europe, either cycling or hitch-hiking, telling his parents he was going to stay with friends. On one trip he travelled with a friend who was interested in cathedrals and they went from one great church to another, marvelling at the engineering skills of the builders and drinking in the spiritual and physical beauty of their creations.

Even as he was exploring England and Europe, he was reading about the plains of Africa and the jungles of South America and wondering how he could get to see and experience more. He was aware that there was a limit to how far he could get on a bike, that such ambitious travel would require money, and he promised himself he would do everything possible to make enough as soon as he could.

CHAPTER FIVE
The Transition Generation

It seems unlikely that Jim's mind ever stops racing. When Sue and I eventually rose the next morning, having lain in bed longer than we should watching the boats going past the windows through the palms, we made our way towards the kitchen in search of some breakfast. He was already sitting at the long glass-topped dining room table next door, bent over his laptop, tapping away, as he waited for us. He had been up since four that morning, unable to still his brain for long enough to sleep, spending the first few hours of the day working on his latest book in the tower at the top of the house that served as his study, a glass of orange juice on the desk in front of him and dawn breaking across the bay below as the first boats started to potter back and forth.

'All I ask', Lillian said, with a twinkle in her eye as we gathered for breakfast, 'is that he visits the real world for at least one hour a day.' Jim had heard and smiled lovingly as he rummaged through the food on display in search of whatever it was he wanted to eat. It seemed likely that it was a conversation they had often. Sue gave me a look that suggested she thought she and Lillian were going to find a lot in common over the next few days, but I pretended not to notice.

'So, what is the book you are working on now?' I asked as we sat down at the suspended glass table and the espresso machine emitted dark steamy aromas.

Jim is always working on a new book. He has published over a hundred, which probably makes him the most prolific academic writer ever, and their international sales form the bedrock of his fortune.

'It's a history of the twenty-first century,' he said, immediately fired with the enthusiasm that makes him such a mesmeric speaker. 'I'm looking back from the year 2100, creating likely scenarios for each of the threads of change between now and then, writing them in the present tense as if they are real, living history.'

The century we are currently living through has become something of a fixation with Jim. It is his belief, along with a number of other very serious scientists and thinkers, that we are entering a period of serious danger (the thrashing white waters at the narrowest part of the imaginary canyon that he was describing the night before). Either this could turn out to be 'our final century' (which is the title of a book by Jim's friend and advisor to The 21st Century School, Martin Rees, who was the Astronomer Royal and is now President of the Royal Society), or it could be the start of the most glorious and exciting period of civilization ever.

'Are you optimistic or pessimistic?' I asked.

'I've spent my life as a person involved in the change of complex systems,' he said. 'If you take the right actions the outcome can be good. If you don't they can go seriously wrong. It needs knowledge and computer modelling to understand what is needed, and then a great deal of education so that people realize what has to be done. Science is needed to understand what is happening, but most politicians haven't a clue about science.

'The great Carl Sagan used to say that the scariest thing of all is "to live in a society dependent on science and technology, where almost no one knows anything about science and technology".

'Young people often ask me what time in history I would live in if I had the choice,' he said, ignoring the food that he had so carefully selected a few moments before, 'expecting me to say the Age of Pericles in Athens perhaps, or the beginning of the Renaissance in Florence, or maybe the height of the Roman Empire, the *belle époque* in Paris or the time of Shakespeare in London, but my answer is always the same. I would choose to be young now, like them, because the next hundred years could be the most exciting time ever to be alive. We are on the brink of unlocking so many new capabilities.'

'Do you think we'll survive this century?' I asked.

'I think I know what we have to do to avoid the catastrophes that are threatening us and how we might work towards building a golden age. But there is no way of knowing whether we will do the right things in time or not. Our heads of state may continue to fiddle while Rome burns.'

At that moment there was a clattering of busy little claws across the tiled floor as Tucker spun crazily through the room from one terrace to another, yelping with joy, heralding the arrival of his master. When Paul eventually followed into the room he was bubbling with excitement at the latest trees and shrubs to burst into springtime bloom and show that they had survived another winter of Atlantic storms and winds.

'The point is,' Jim continued, once Paul and Tucker had passed through, having given him a chance to pause and eat, 'technology is becoming powerful enough to wreck the planet, but it is also going to have the power to transform everything and give us the most spectacular future. Now is a wonderful time to be young.

'The big question is, can we produce the people of wisdom that we need to lead us through this transition and to build this great civilization? Most of the degrees that universities are offering now won't achieve that because so many subjects have become so complex. We are teaching subjects in incredible depth and constantly measuring how much the students are learning. They are coming out of the universities with much narrower and deeper knowledge of their individual subjects, but with less general, widespread knowledge that could be transformed into wisdom.'

'So how do you define wisdom?' I asked, happy to coax him to keep talking while I ate.

'Wisdom is the capability to look at wide-ranging situations and put all the various pieces into a sensible pattern, getting information to work with that pattern and making the right decisions. It usually comes later in life, when you have learned lessons in many different areas and can take a more multidisciplinary approach to problems, creating a synthesis of a broad range of knowledge in order to reach wise decisions.

'The problem is that specialists tend to develop their own languages: doctors, biologists, sociologists and physicists all talk in different tongues. If we can teach them all the language of mathematics they can suddenly communicate with extreme precision. That is partly what I wanted to achieve with the setting up of The 21st Century School – a more multidisciplinary approach to the future, in which brilliant people in different disciplines can work together. Ultimately it's all about finding and supporting brilliant people.

'The lack of wisdom that we have shown over the last half century in the way we have dealt with nuclear weapons is a good example of how stupid the cleverest people can be. We were very lucky not to have destroyed the world with our incredible inventions and discoveries, and we can't afford to take any more risks like that, not now we have such awesome capabilities for destruction.

'Technology has changed history far more dramatically than politics in the last three centuries. We have had the arrival of steam engines, ships, railways, telephones, cars, planes, atomic bombs and computers. During the twenty-first century we will have far more radical developments than any of those and we are going to have to re-think the way we do everything.'

Jim's attention was distracted to the window that surrounded us and looked out over a wall of water that plunged into the overgrown ponds of the quarry garden way below. A longtail, an elegantly plumed white bird peculiar to Bermuda, swooped in to one of the nests that had been specially built into the quarry wall opposite. Jim watched her for a moment, lost in thought.

'She'll wait there now until a male comes to find her,' he said eventually as he sipped his coffee, all thoughts of Armageddon apparently put aside for the simple pleasure of watching a beautiful bird in flight. 'I set up lights in one of the nests one year and filmed the whole mating ritual. They didn't seem to be remotely concerned by the intrusion. We've had experts here building nesting boxes all over the island, disguising them in the cliffs.'

Tom Martin couldn't understand why his son would want even to consider going to a place like Oxford. It was so far away to start with, and would be full of the sort of rich idiots he most despised. What would be the point of such an education for a boy who daydreamed all the time and didn't seem to be suited to any normal job anyway? Tom's most fundamental worry, however, despite the headmaster's assurances that everything would be taken care of, was how could a family like his ever afford to send their son to such a place?

'You don't have to worry about that, Mr Martin,' the headmaster had assured him. 'Jim is going to be going for a scholarship. If the university accepts him they will be paying for everything.'

Although this robbed Tom of his only really valid objection to the whole process, he remained stubbornly unconvinced about the whole thing right to the end. Mabel, as usual, said nothing, apparently willing to let fate take its inevitable course.

Under his headmaster's careful guidance, Jim did a three-month crash course in Latin (every applicant had to take an advanced exam in the language, confirming Tom's opinion that the whole thing was mad and pointless), and applied to several colleges. He was invited down to Oxford for two weeks of interviews, unsure of what exactly was expected of him or what they would be looking for. He was a shy provincial boy wading into waters far out of his depth, while relishing every strange and exotic moment he got to spend amongst the dreaming spires and historic panelled rooms.

Many years later he discovered that the professors and dons had been looking for something very specific during those two weeks of seemingly relaxed conversations and cocktail parties, interspersed with requests for the applicants to write essays with titles such as 'If seagulls were as intelligent as people, what sort of cities would they build?' and 'How would you persuade an intelligent man that the earth is round?'

At one stage Jim was asked to draw an 'ampersand'. Never having heard this term, which describes the sign (&) representing 'and', he spent an hour drawing a rocket-propelled machine that travelled on caterpillar tracks and bristled with weather vanes and satellite antennae, radar dishes, robotic arms and a Wurlitzer. Only later did he discover that his artwork had ended up pinned to the notice board of the senior common room.

'We were always looking for people who we thought would do something interesting, extraordinary and different with their lives,' a don later explained to him. 'We weren't as worried then about what exam results a boy might have achieved at school.'

Following the two weeks of interviews and essay writing, Jim was offered a place to study physics at Keble College. Tom still couldn't see the point of any of it, but nothing could possibly have discouraged Jim now that he had tasted life amongst like-minded thinkers and academics.

In the 1950s the majority of students at Oxford and Cambridge still came from wealthy families. At least that was how it seemed to Jim as he arrived at the station and walked to the college carrying all his worldly belongings, including the telescope he had made from cardboard, which afforded him a better view of the night sky than anything Galileo had ever had. He could imagine these fellow students living in the sorts of houses that he and his friends had broken into and walked around in wide-eyed wonder. He felt none of the resentment that was common towards the rich at that time, merely a growing curiosity about what their lives might be like, and a feeling that he would like to be a part of that world of beautiful houses and broader horizons, if he could just find a way.

It was a time of great optimism. A young Queen ascended the throne and her Coronation become the first major television event broadcast in the country. Mount Everest was climbed for the first time in 1953 and just a few years later President Kennedy would be announcing that America was planning to put a man on the moon. Such magnificent ideas made Jim's head spin with the possibilities of what excitements might lie ahead for a bright young scientist.

His unmodernized rooms, which were off an ancient stone staircase and which he shared with one other man, were spacious and panelled in oak. They came with enough shelving for several hundred books, a fireplace and servant, or 'scout', to light it each morning and keep it stocked with coal. The scout was also required to supply a jug of hot water each morning for washing and to make the men's beds. Jim was impressed by the ingenuity that their scout *showed in supplying any service he was asked for (provided he was fairly tipped). The antiquated rules of the university were still written in Latin and one instructed that 'gentlemen will not fly airplanes within twenty miles of Halifax'. The authorities had even managed to find a Latin word for 'airplane'.*

Evelyn Waugh's infamous novel Brideshead Revisited, *based on his time at Oxford thirty years earlier, had been out for about eight years by then and it was fashionable to pretend that nothing had changed in the rarefied world where aristocracy and academia came together. Jim even went out for a while with a girl who carried a teddy bear called Aloysius around, just like Waugh's fictional hero Lord Sebastian Flyte.*

Although he couldn't compete socially, having no money beyond his scholarship fund, Jim was determined not to miss out on any of the experiences on offer and invested in a second-hand tuxedo so that he would be able to attend all the balls and formal events, discovering the joys of dancing the night away whenever the efforts of making small talk had finally become too much. He began to learn about the worlds of hunting, sailing, fishing and partying.

It was like being part of some grand and ancient piece of theatre, but it was soon obvious to Jim, and other working-class lads from the north, that they were going to have to lose their local accents if they wanted to be understood and if they wanted to move easily amongst those who spoke 'the Queen's English'. Jim reserved his Ashby-de-la-Zouche accent to bring out purely as a party piece. His transformation was now well underway.

Although no one ever held his lack of money against him, Jim saw how wealthier undergraduates were able to throw champagne parties and fill their girlfriends' rooms with roses, and how they took skiing holidays and owned second homes in places like Portugal. Although he never doubted his own ability to lead an interesting life, there were times when he thought he might have to accept that he would never be able to make the sort of money needed to live like these people. He was determined, however, to take every opportunity that was offered to him to sample the good life while he could.

Owning the evening suit meant that he was also able to go to hunt balls when he returned home during the vacations. He had always enjoyed the spectacle of the famous Quorn Hunt and used to go to the meets to admire the grand society ladies riding side-saddle in their silk top hats and long black riding habits. Although his debilitating shyness and lack of finance had meant romance was initially kept tantalizingly beyond his reach at Oxford, when he returned to Ashby-de-la-Zouche he found that his newly acquired layer of gloss, however thin it might still be, was already paying off and he acquired a girlfriend called Gabriela.

Gabriela was a sturdy young woman and a member of the Young Farmers' Association who ran a chicken farm and also rode with the hunt, which gave Jim access to invitations to the hunt balls. Gabriela had the added advantage of owning a pick-up truck with a mattress in the back. Even on the nights of the balls, however, the chickens still had to be rounded up and she and Jim could be spotted in full evening dress trying to coax recalcitrant fowls out of trees with their umbrellas. Although such antics would have confirmed every dire warning Tom had ever uttered on the idiocy of the upper classes, Jim was becoming increasingly entranced by the infinite variety of the life that was opening up in front of him.

Forced to take whatever work he could find during the vacations in order to give himself a little spare money for the following term, Jim worked for a while at a local biscuit factory, standing on the assembly line, watching for broken or misshapen biscuits that needed to be picked out. The din of the machinery was overwhelming after the peace and tranquillity of Oxford, the women around him having to screech to make themselves heard, and everywhere he looked Jim saw nothing but mesmerizing, dehumanizing boredom. People were treated like mere cogs and now that he was experiencing it at first hand he couldn't believe that his family and their friends took it for granted that this was to be their lot in life, that there couldn't be a better future. The misery of those weeks made him all the more determined to milk every possible drop of goodness from the educational opportunities he was being offered.

Although he was confident that he would be able to avoid ending up standing on a production line by then, he knew there were many other tedious, soul-destroying jobs just waiting to suck him in. Mental drudgery, he was sure, could be worse than physical drudgery if it left you with no space to daydream.

The ethos of the time in the grander universities like Oxford was to encourage students to follow their interests and take full advantage of everything that was on offer, and Jim didn't need to be told twice, attending exhibitions and concerts and soaking up every scrap of art and music and culture that he could find.

He discovered that world-famous figures such as CS Lewis, Isaiah Berlin and Bertrand Russell were still lecturing and he made a point of seeking them out. Bertrand Russell particularly intrigued him and he would sit at the great man's feet, sipping tea or sherry and asking questions for as long as Russell was willing to answer them.

'I'm eighty-two years old', the old philosopher would squeak in his distinctive, reedy voice, 'and I can still learn faster than any of you can. Why?' He looked around for a response. 'Because I am a professional learner. I have spent my whole life learning how to learn. So my brain is accustomed to taking in new ideas and information very fast.'

His words stayed with Jim, who was to spend the next half century honing his own thinking and imaginative abilities in just the same way, although at that stage he had no idea what he was going to do with his life or how he was going to make use of the education that had fallen into his lap.

Many of the lectures that he attended on subjects like physics and engineering led him to believe that the world was on the verge of changes every bit as radical as those brought by the Industrial Revolution a century before. He was becoming more and more intrigued by the subject of computers and the possibilities that they seemed to be opening up, but his professors were less impressed: such matters were still considered outside the world of respectable academia.

Unable to face the prospect of going back to the biscuit factory, Jim asked the university's appointments board to try to find him something better when the next vacation came round. They helped him to find work in the laboratories of United Steel, researching into X-ray crystallography, which meant he was now meeting other scientists.

When Jim was due to receive his bachelor's degree Tom and Mabel nervously agreed to come down to Oxford for the ceremony, which was to be held in the Sheldonian Theatre, one of the most beautiful buildings in Oxford. It was a four-hour ceremony conducted in Latin. Tom fell soundly asleep and snored loudly while Mabel smiled her sweet, kind smile and said she hoped Jim wasn't getting 'out of his depth'. Both of them declined to repeat the experience when Jim was later presented with his Master's degree.

For a time, Jim was a rocket scientist, doing research on combustion in rocket motors. An attempt was being made to develop a rocket motor that was small but extremely powerful but it was causing overheating problems that would sometimes melt the walls of the combustion chamber. The heat flow in the combustion chamber was simulated in a large vat of molten wax. When it was announced that the Duke of Edinburgh was to visit the laboratory total panic ensued. The place was cleaned top-to-toe, and cynical, bearded researchers were made to wear ties. To Jim's horror, the bath of wax had been unplugged and the wax had solidified. He quickly plugged in its heater but it took hours to re-melt the wax and only part of it was liquid by the time a convoy of Rolls Royces pulled up outside. As the Duke was being ushered into the building the wax was expanding as it melted, putting steadily growing pressure on the still-solid wax at the top. As the Royal party approached, molten wax burst through the top and shot up like the geysers in Yellowstone Park, coating the entire room, all the equipment and research assistants in hot, dripping wax. The Duke was speedily diverted.

Although he was sure he would enjoy dedicating his life to research work, Jim was horrified to discover how badly scientists were paid. However hard he thought about it he couldn't come up with a formula that would give him a chance to do interesting work and make enough money to explore the world in the way he wanted. The lack of money at home that he had taken for granted when he was a child was now starkly obvious to him when he returned having seen more of the world. He could see how it had entrapped his parents and he was determined to find a way to avoid the same fate befalling him.

One of the ambitions that exposure to Oxford had ignited in Jim was an urge to write. He had contributed to magazines at university and the college Dean gave him a copy of Evelyn Waugh's novel Scoop, *a satire on the world of newspaper reporting in which journalists brazenly invented their stories. He hadn't liked fiction much up till then, but Waugh's comic skills and way with words inspired him to write two novels himself. The first was a comic book about Oxford life and the second a science fiction story about aliens. He even got as far as catching the attention of a London literary agent before the inevitable rejection slips started to come in and his writing career stalled, like so many other bright young people both before and after him. Although he soon realized that neither of these books was ever going to be published, the experience did not put Jim off. He wanted to write and promised himself that sooner or later he would find a way to publication.*

Jim was becoming obsessed with the idea that society was about to change beyond recognition and would ask friends at Oxford who were steeped in the classics what they thought civilization ought to be like and how technology ought to be used.

'What does it mean to be civilized?' he asked. 'What should be the characteristics of a great civilization?'

'A society', one replied, 'where boredom is a crime.'

'The development of the mind to enjoy the most subtle pleasures,' said another.

'Development of the intellect to its maximum capability.'

'A society of maximum creativity.'

'Blondes, bikinis, open sports cars and Californian sunshine.'

CHAPTER SIX
The Singularity

Once breakfast had finished Sue asked if it would be alright for her to go and ask Paul some questions about the gardens. She'd noticed the previous evening that he had attached lovingly inscribed name tags to many of the plants and she sensed she had found a valuable source of information for her own gardening ambitions back in the milder climes of Sussex.

'He'll love to have someone show an interest,' Lillian assured her. 'He has to spend an awful lot of time here on his own with no one but the manic Tucker for company.'

Lillian then disappeared into her own office with her laptop to catch up on anything happening in the outside world that she might need to bring to Jim's attention and Sue strolled outside, leaving us with the coffee machine. Lillian is a relentless researcher in all the subjects that Jim needs to know about.

A smiling and benign Nepalese woman worked quietly around us as we talked, doing household chores.

'I can never remember her name,' Jim confessed when she was out of earshot, 'so I have to call her Kathmandu. She rolls our clothes up into tight little bundles like she's packing for a yak trip.'

'Do you fancy a walk?' he enquired after we'd been talking for a while.

There was no sign of Sue, Paul or Tucker as we made our way down yet another set of steps I hadn't noticed before, pushing back the encroaching plants every few paces.

'It wasn't until after I'd bought the island and we were clearing some of the undergrowth with chainsaws that we realized there was something strange going on underground,' Jim explained as he led me past several gardens and through a curved brick entrance into a narrow alleyway apparently cut into the rock. The walls stretched up twenty-five feet above our heads to fern-covered slats, which had been inserted to stop people falling to their deaths from the gardens above, allowing through only strips of light and none of the warmth from outside.

'The first things we found were some ancient decorative stone towers with shafts that seemed to go deep down into the rock. When we shouted down them we could hear a long echo. As we cut back further around them we found a sort of pyramid of stairs, like stone terraces, all covered in lush asparagus fern. Then we found these overgrown stone doorways into spaces that were filled with the debris of at least a century. It was like uncovering a lost city. The more we cleared the further we discovered these man-made tunnels and stairways stretched into the rocks beneath the island. It was like opening up the tombs of Egypt, although the only corpse we found belonged to some poor dog who must have got locked in some time in the last century or two.'

Eventually Jim and his fellow explorers cut their way into what looked like the entrance to a British railway tunnel, which opened up into the subterranean passage we were now standing in.

Jim led the way to a door and opened it. Inside it was pitch black. Fiddling around for a light switch, he suddenly illuminated a huge underground area in front of us with ten arched chambers built with the same immaculate brickwork as the curved entrances outside. Before me was the astonishing sight of more than twelve thousand square feet of underground vaults.

'All these bricks must have been shipped over from England by the British', Jim said, leading the way down the towering corridor past the arches, 'so that the convicts could build this underground gunpowder store. The amazing thing is that it was kept totally and absolutely secret. We checked all the historical records and there is no mention of this place anywhere. The computers in the Greenwich Maritime Museum have every detail about every nut and bolt in every military installation in Bermuda, but there's no mention of this – and it's the biggest British gunpowder store in the Western hemisphere. I checked the records of the Governor of Bermuda – no mention of it. No mention of the entire island. Nobody in Bermuda knows it's here, but just look at it!'

Jim stopped at one of the ten vaults, now lit and air conditioned, the gentle breeze circulating through from the dark passages outside.

'When Rudy Giuliani was on the Presidential trail in 2007', he said, 'he wanted somewhere where he could entertain the billionaires at an insurance conference in Bermuda, who were potential donors to his campaign. He wanted to keep the meeting secret and secure and someone had told him about this place, so he asked if he could put on a dinner for them here. A dining room was set up for forty guests. They installed an entire French kitchen in here, complete with a jovial French chef in a huge chef's hat. I was talking to him and his chef's smock fell aside slightly, and he had a pistol tucked into his belt. Bermuda allows absolutely no guns. The police don't have guns. He was no ordinary chef. I found out later that there were twelve security people.

'It was strictly a men-only event. I sat next to Giuliani. He brandished a huge Cuban cigar and told everybody "This'd be illegal in New York." Late in the evening he asked where my wife was. I told him she was on the island and he said "Get her down here." Duncan had a camera in the shadows with a powerful telephoto lens. I have wonderful photographs of Lillian whispering in Giuliani's ear, looking exactly like Lady Macbeth plotting his rise to power. Instead of giving me orders, as usual, she was telling him what to do when he was President of the USA.

'You know,' he said as we made our way back out into the passageway, past a sentry box where red-coated soldiers would have stood guard a hundred and twenty years before, 'human nature hasn't really changed since Shakespeare's time. We have the same Lady Macbeths, the same power struggles, the same greed, love, kindness, jealousy and treachery as in his day. The chances are it won't change much in the next four hundred years either, but everything else will change.'

Leading me up a long flight of underground steps we came out into a cool, mature, subterranean water garden filled with orchids and tree ferns from New Zealand, exotic lilies from Australia and spiky blue aristae from South Africa. It had once been yet another of the eight or more quarries that pitted the island, but was now covered in a dome of slats to make a Javanese roof and we sat down beside more ponds filled with koi carp. The air was kept moist by water falling around us from above the pillars and arches.

'The thing that people need to understand', Jim said after a while, 'is that The Singularity will become a reality in the coming years.'

'I'm sorry ...' I had a horrible feeling I might have missed something, like those times at school when you would discover you had daydreamed through some vital bit of the teacher's explanation, that you had left it too late to ask and that nothing was going to make sense from now on. 'What is "The Singularity" exactly?'

One of the reasons Jim is possibly the most successful teacher in the world is because he has endless patience and is always willing to re-explain something to the slowest in the class.

'It is a break in human evolution that will be caused by the staggering speed of technological evolution,' he said, pausing to allow his words to sink in. 'Computers are increasing in power at a rate of a thousand every fifteen years. In thirty-five years time, the largest computer will be able to execute a thousand billion billion operations per second. It will have about a thousand billion billion bytes of memory. An unbelievable amount of computing power. Networks will grow in capacity at about the same rate. By 2040 we will have a global network with almost every major computer connected to it. The control mechanisms will allow very large jobs to be shared among computers on the global network – more than a hundred million computers if necessary.

'Computer intelligence will grow immensely beyond human intelligence, but will be fundamentally different from it.'

I looked down at the fish flickering past below my feet and tried to get my head around what he was saying, but I wasn't sure it was possible. There were a few scenarios I needed explaining in more detail.

'So what will that mean to the people in the street?' I asked.

'It means that the machines will be cleverer than us and will continue multiplying their capability at an unimaginable speed. It will change the rules of our game.

'It's already happening. The way to generate wealth is becoming increasingly technical. Real-time networks are on line to one another instantly, all part of the production processes. Singularity will make this process even more fiercely complex and instantaneous. A set of countries will be linked electronically into a "real-time club", but other countries will not be part of it. The most treacherous part of the canyon that humanity is heading into will coincide with the arrival of The Singularity and with the serious impacts of global warming.'

He fell quiet again for a moment, lost in thought.

'If we understand this century and learn how to play its very complex game', he said eventually, 'our future will be magnificent. If we get it wrong, we may be at the start of a new type of Dark Age.'

I felt I had been duly warned and shivered a little as he led me up yet another staircase out of the subterranean water garden and into the cloister overlooking the cheerful quadrangle at the centre of the house and leading to the kitchen. The glass table was spread with yet another meal. It sounded like Lillian and Sue were exchanging confidences as we came in.

'Paul is amazing,' Sue enthused as we sat down. 'He's built benches all over the island, using logs and driftwood and anything he can find to decorate them. They're all placed to give the most incredible views. It's like an art form in itself. There's even a figure built in the undergrowth made from driftwood that he calls "Agar Man". It's like a theatrical performance. He says there are more than forty seats dotted around in hidden places. I'm going to find them all and photograph them. It'll be my project.'

Having been talking all morning, Jim settled into a comfortable silence as he ate his lunch, tuning out the rest of us, allowing us to prattle on as he watched benignly, apparently withdrawing into his own thoughts and preparing himself to work through the afternoon.

After lunch Sue took me on a tour of Paul's benches and we ended up sitting on a beach in a small, sandy bay. A miniature stone fortress, which a century earlier had been a latrine for British officers, acted as a changing room so that I could pull on a swimming costume and slide into the clear, cool water. Rolling on to my back I floated out towards the reefs and squinted up at the house and Jim's tower stretching away into the blue sky, fancying that I could discern movement as he worked in his armchair in the window, bent over his laptop, striving to understand everything before it was too late.

🌐

All young British men in the 1950s had to do <u>two years of military service</u> and so it was that after years of living in the idyllic surrounds of Oxford Jim found himself on a drill square being treated like the scum of the earth by a sergeant who referred to him as 'Rocket-Bonce' and yelled that the lolloping six-foot-five mal-coordinated recruit 'marched like a pregnant fairy'.

Most of his grander friends had assumed they would automatically be made officers and received a nasty shock when they discovered that wasn't always going to be the case. Jim, on the other hand, had no illusions. He didn't expect to be spotted as officer material so he had spent a great deal of time finding out exactly how to get a Commission. While the majority of soldiers lived lives of tedium and drudgery he could see that officers could live and dine in grand style, even having their own servants, or 'batmen'. The prospect of wasting two valuable years of his life 'square bashing' was unthinkable – he had to find a way to spend the time profitably and interestingly. He was also convinced that if he could become an officer it would help him when he came to apply for managerial jobs at the end of the two years.

To make the jump to the good life, however, he knew he was going to have to prove he had leadership qualities. Given how quietly spoken, shy and tongue-tied he was, he realized that was not going to be easy. As usual he went back to reading in search of a solution, having discovered a dry tome entitled The Group Approach to Leadership Testing. *He studied it so hard he virtually learned it off by heart and then fell back on the acting skills he had first discovered at school.*

The Army agreed to let him try out and he was sent on ten days of tests at the War Office Selection Board, many of them to do with problem solving, which was very much his strength, and miraculously he passed.

'But you couldn't tell a rifle from a bleedin' pitchfork!' his sergeant complained when he heard the news.

What Jim didn't know was that his tutor at Oxford, a famous physicist called Roger Blin-Stoyle, had written to the selection board to tell them that Jim's specialty at university had been sub-atomic particle physics. The selection board suggested that he should work for his two years of National Service on the hydrogen bomb and behind the scenes the authorities were in the process of security clearing him.

One particularly unpleasant day Jim was out on an exercise, lying flat in wet ferns with a machine gun firing blanks at an imaginary enemy.

'James Martin?' a voice enquired.

Jim turned to see what looked like a City gentleman, complete with black bowler hat and briefcase, standing over him.

'Yes?'

The man explained he was involved in the security clearance process and continued to ask questions, standing bolt upright and taking notes as the mock war raged in the undergrowth around him. The man then went away and Jim continued with his training.

A few days before he was due to be awarded his Commission by Field Marshal Lord Montgomery as part of a grand passing out parade, a large, black, ministerial Humber full of men in bowler hats drove on to the parade ground and announced that they had come to take Jim to Aldermaston, which was then the centre of nuclear weapons research in

Britain. They bundled him into the car and whisked him away.

'But I'm passing out in a few days' time,' he protested, not wanting to miss out on the event he had been working towards through six months of hell. 'Can't it wait till then?'

'You will not get a Commission,' they informed him. 'You will be living as a civilian and doing physics research.'

By that stage Jim had set his heart on getting his Commission and begged them to let him continue, explaining that a Commission would help his career once he left the Army.

'Don't worry,' they tried to reassure him. 'From now on your life will be very different. You are going to live in comfort and work with some of the brightest physicists in the world.'

They kept up with the psychological pressure for two days.

'There comes a time in everyone's life when they have to decide whether or not they will do something for their country,' he was told. 'Now is the time for you to address that issue. What do you say, Mr Martin?'

'Take me back so that I can get my Commission?'

'Do you have any moral objections to working on the bomb, Mr Martin?'

'No, I have no moral objections,' Jim said, still unsure what his views on such subjects were, 'but I want to receive my Commission first.'

'You have two choices.' The man was obviously becoming exasperated. 'Either you stay here, live in comfort and work as a researcher for the remainder of your two years or else you go back for your Commission and serve as a very junior officer.'

By this stage Jim had completely convinced himself that an Army Commission would help him get a good job in management.

'Take me back to the Officer Cadet School.'

Ten days later he received his Commission from Field Marshal Montgomery. He was then sent on a dispatch riders' course and given an 800cc motorbike. Back at the British Legion in Ashby-de-la-Zouche, Tom Martin and his drinking friends found the latest twists in his son's life completely baffling.

CHAPTER SEVEN
Eco-Affluence and the Happy List

'Look at this!' Jim could hardly contain his glee the next morning as he beckoned us to look at whatever he had found on his laptop in the early hours of the day. 'A friend has sent it through.'

The link he had been sent took him to an article that had appeared in *The Independent on Sunday* in England. The editors had compiled something they were calling 'The Happy List', an antidote to 'The Rich List' published the same day by their rivals *The Sunday Times*. The list comprised of a hundred people who had made Britain a better place to live in, whose prime motive was to make the lives of strangers happier. Several of them, including Jim, were multi-millionaires who had chosen to give their money away rather than storing it up in order to qualify for the *Sunday Times* list.

There is a general perception, frequently reinforced by the media, that predictions of the future are all about doom and gloom. Stories of overpopulation, dwindling resources, global warming, increasing poverty, crime and violence dominate the headlines, and futurologists like Jim are often quoted as predicting that things will be getting steadily worse from now on, that we cannot continue to grow and become more affluent because the planet cannot sustain our endless appetites. It was encouraging to see a newspaper pointing out the fact that Jim, and others like him, is actually optimistic about the future and thinks it could be an infinitely better place in which to live than the past ever was.

'I coined the phrase "eco-affluence" a while ago,' he said, 'and I still stand by it. It's perfectly possible for us to immensely improve our lifestyles and enjoy our lives more without using up an unsustainable share of the planet's resources. There can be new lifestyles of the grandest quality that heal rather than harm our global ecosystem.

'To be able to live with clean water and beautiful gardens around us, for instance, is infinitely more desirable than spending our lives slaving on factory assembly lines or driving cars along motorways day in and day out just to make a bit more money so we can buy more material goods. To be able to watch any movie you want whenever you want, to have time to listen to wonderful music or to read and write books. There are so many ways of being affluent without harming the environment – in fact improving the environment. Some involve the love of nature, some involve high technology and some involve opera, football, or jazz. You could be interested in ocean racing, paragliding, bird watching, hydroponics, cricket, camping or three-dimensional chess. With the use of earphones and 3D goggles we can take state-of-the-art entertainment anywhere we want it. The earth will soon have large protected hotspots of immense biodiversity, and some people will be passionate about understanding and expanding this biodiversity.

'There will be a near-infinite number of eco-affluent avocations, such as the study of theatre, breeding genetically modified orchids, practising classical Indian sitar performances. The twenty-first century will bring extraordinary levels of eco-affluent creativity. To avoid playing havoc with the planet, we need eco-affluence to become highly fashionable, worldwide.

'The generation that will bear the brunt of all the challenges and change in the first half of the twenty-first century will be those born, say, between 1985 and 2015. I call them the Transition Generation, or "T-Generation".'

'So you wouldn't include Corinthia in the T-Generation?' I asked.

'No. Too old. But your daughters are. They will be part of the greatest transition in human history. They will form the counterbalance to all the relentless downward indicators. Their spirit, energy and optimism will lead to changed civilizations. At the moment people fear that environmental correctness will slow down economies, but that generation will be turning it into opportunities for new eco-affluent growth.'

As we went through to organize some breakfast Jim kept talking, unable to keep his own enthusiasm in check for even a moment.

'The growth of a nation's economy has become disconnected from the happiness of its citizens, and that doesn't make sense. We need a world in which economic growth is synonymous with growth in the quality of life.

'Paul's got it right,' he said, spotting Paul working on a tree in the distance with Tucker sitting below, staring up at his master with quivering adoration. 'He's worked out that he enjoys creating sculptures from driftwood, so he's found a job that allows him to do it.

'The first step for anyone is to work out what they enjoy doing in life,' he continued, pouring himself some juice. 'Since the dawn of television advertising, the whole Western world has been swept along by a deliberate policy of making everyone envious of their neighbours, insecure about their status, and desperate to acquire more material goods. "Keeping up with the Joneses" is one of the most damaging philosophies ever invented. One man builds a triple garage and buys another car and so his next-door neighbour, who until that moment was perfectly contented with his one car and single garage, believes he has to do the same. The cost of building this structure and filling it with cars means he has to borrow money, and has to work more hours in order to pay the interest on that borrowed money. His quality of life is instantly diminished, which is the exact opposite of what he has been promised by the advertisers of cars and garages. If he had realized at the start that he actually enjoyed having more leisure time and less stress he would have seen that giving that up was not a good price to pay simply for having a bigger garage.

'If I were trying to keep up with my neighbours out there' – he waved vaguely out the window at the multi-millionaire mansions dotted around the coastlines across the bay – 'I would have to buy a private jet and a three-masted schooner, but what a headache that would be. I'd rather have a subscription to Netflix, have my fourteen-foot Blu-ray wall screen and go to some really great concerts. Duncan likes sailing around the island on his boat so he lives in a dock house.

'The young instinctively know that they should do what they enjoy as long as it doesn't harm anyone else. The motivation of the kids who created the internet music revolution was not to make money – it was to provide digital freedom and to give people the music they enjoy the most. They believed that total freedom of information should be built into the internet so that you can download what you want, free of high charges, free of censorship, free from attacks by lawyers. Eventually some sort of charging structure had to evolve, but it was a much fairer one than would have been the case if everything on the internet were designed to maximize profit. Hopefully the T-Generation will continue to innovate in the same way because it is the right thing to do, not because it is necessarily the profitable thing to do. For many, understanding the meaning of the twenty-first century will give meaning to their own lives.'

Getting on to the 'Happy List' is by no means the first time Jim has been honoured. In 2007 he won *The Guardian*

Award for safeguarding the planet from The Lifeboat Foundation. The following year the same award went to Stephen Hawking and in previous years to Warren Buffett, Martin Rees, Ray Kurzweil (the founder of The Singularity University in California) and Prince Charles.

The Lifeboat Foundation is a non-profit, non-governmental organization dedicated to encouraging scientific advancements while helping humanity to survive the many risks to its existence and possible misuse of increasingly powerful technologies, including genetic engineering, nanotechnology, robotics and artificial intelligence as we move towards a technological singularity. Oxford awarded Jim the Sheldon medal, which is on display in the Ashmolean museum. Britain's ancient and prestigious Royal Institute made him an honorary lifetime Fellow. He is a Fellow of the World Academy of Art and Science. He is also a Senior Fellow of the James Martin Center for Non-Proliferation Studies at Monterey, California, the largest non-governmental organization devoted exclusively to research and training on nonproliferation issues.

'How many honorary doctorates do you have from universities now?' I asked as the list kept rolling on.

'I've lost count, I'm afraid, but I do know they have come from all six continents, which I am proud of.' His business card read: James Martin MA, D.Litt, Hon D.Sc, Hon D.Eng, Hon Ph.D, Hon LLD, Hon D.HL, FWAAS.

In the 1950s the British Army was attempting to keep the peace in the civil war raging in Cyprus and was regularly under attack by terrorists when Jim found himself shipped out to join the 43rd Light Anti-Aircraft Regiment, who had responsibility for security around Nicosia.

As a humble Engineering Officer, Jim was left pretty much to his own devices on a day-to-day basis. An

Engineering Officer was considered a lower order of creature than the Gunner Officers, but Jim still managed to get the men in the workshops to lay a concrete floor in his tent, which the Gunner Officers didn't have, and to fit all sorts of electrical luxuries. He invented an insect-killing machine, which used a pin-point of light to attract insects into the sharp blades of a fan, where they were instantly sliced up. He then sold these devices to the Gunner Officers.

His reputation as a photographer led to him being ordered to undertake reconnaissance photography from the air, climbing out on to the wing struts of a small single-engine plane. He had a large camera with film that could be magnified greatly to help the intelligence service search for terrorist activity. Still little more than a kid, he relished the excitement of climbing outside the plane while it was in flight, tethered only by a harness.

Although he was still impatient to get out into the world and earn a living, the posting to Cyprus did allow him to broaden his horizons and helped him to develop his confidence in dealing with other people. He was never going to be a natural commander of men, but he was at least learning some very basic leadership skills and enjoying himself at the same time.

Travelling to Baghdad with a friend from Oxford during a month's leave, he lived in a mud hut perched precariously on the roof of a derelict building in the centre of the city at a time when the Iraqi royal family was brutally hung drawn and quartered, a medieval form of execution and torture. Rioting crowds burned down the British Embassy and the two friends ended up having to escape to Tehran disguised as pilgrims. Jim almost gave the game away when his good manners got the better of him and he stood up to offer his seat on a bus to a woman, insulting her husband's manhood in the process.

Despite the bus breaking down in the snow-covered mountains, leaving the passengers huddled round a hastily built fire, they eventually made it to Tehran where they were welcomed into a lavish expatriate lifestyle, which was a stark contrast to the medieval brutality that was going on on the other side of the mountains.

By the time his two years of military service were over Jim was even more convinced that he never wanted to lead a dull life, but at the same time he knew he needed to earn a living and build a career if he were to stand any chance of enjoying the sort of good life that he had now seen glimpses of. Although he was deeply nervous of ending up trapped in a job he didn't enjoy, like Tom, there was no option but to start applying to companies, and a few weeks later he was on the verge of signing up as a junior manager with Wiggins Teape, a venerable old British paper company.

'You're making the right decision,' the personnel director assured him as he slid the employment contract across the desk. 'Much better to work for a good, cricket-playing British company than one of these flashy American sharks. They may pay more money, but money isn't everything, is it?'

Jim glanced up from the contract. 'What sort of flashy American organization?' he asked, innocently, alarm bells ringing in his head at the thought of having to turn out for the company cricket team, a tedious and time-wasting activity he had hoped he would never have to endure again after leaving school.

'Oh, you know, people like IBM.'

'May I take this away to study?' Jim asked, folding the contract into his pocket. 'I'll let you know my final decision tomorrow.'

Once out of the office he hurried to a phone box, looked up IBM in the directory and rang them. He was invited in for a series of interviews and was eventually taken on as an Electronic Data Processing Analyst. Contrary to what he had been told, they were actually paying less that Wiggins Teape, but some instinct deep inside Jim's gut told him that this was a company that was going to be exciting to work for, and that he wouldn't at any stage be required to play cricket in order to further his career. There was an air of excitement about the place that suggested that this was not simply a company making 'business machines'.

IBM was run by a family of Quakers called Watson. Two brothers had been in charge since their father, Thomas Watson Senior, had retired. Thomas J Watson ran the USA-based operation and Arthur K Watson took care of the rest of the world. At that stage neither of the brothers had the least idea that their company was working in areas that would change the world so dramatically, but Jim, a raw recruit, had an inkling of what might be about to happen, even though he wasn't yet sure how it would come about.

CHAPTER EIGHT
The Movies

'Shall we watch the movie?' Jim asked that evening, leading the way into a small, darkened cinema area, curtained off from the rest of the library.

I knew exactly which movie he meant. It was a project he had been working on for several years, the movie version of his book *The Meaning of the 21st Century*. The process of filming it had taken him all over the world with a selection of cameramen.

'The first one was like a drunk under a lamppost,' he remembered. 'The second was a martinet for discipline.'

With some tough-guy minders to look after them they got inside shanty towns like the one depicted in *Slumdog Millionaire*. They camped on the Greenland ice cap and suffered a million mosquito bites in the Amazon forests. They travelled to the Aral Sea in the ex-USSR, to a place where there's not a toilet within a hundred miles, and filmed a collection of large ships sitting in a desert with camels wandering amongst them and no humans in sight.

'It was as though these big ships had dropped from the sky,' Jim recalled, 'like a scene from a science fiction film. It is the worst environmental catastrophe that humans have created so far. The fishing towns are now separated from the sea by what looks like a salty moonscape. You couldn't even see the water any more.'

In one shot Jim was walking across what looked like ice, when suddenly he fell through it. It wasn't ice – it was crystallized salt, and the water he fell into was hot.

Jim filmed long, in-depth interviews with many of the most distinguished thinkers about the future from James Lovelock to Martin Rees, from Chris Patten to Nicholas Stern, and Ray Kurzweil to Craig Venter – about seventy in all. Not only does the film contain the ideas that Jim believes in most passionately, it is also a showcase for the writing and film-making skills that he has been honing for decades. Like all great presenters of specialized subjects he brings a lifetime of experience and an enthusiasm that borders on the obsessive to the project, delivering his lines with all the authority you would expect from an expert who has written his own script and with the showmanship of a shy man who only really opens up when he is in front of an audience or a camera. He even presents one argument while driving a car at ridiculous speed over a hairpin bend mountain pass. The resulting film, written, presented and directed by Jim and narrated by Michael Douglas, was about to be shown at the Cannes Film Festival.

Michael Douglas and his film-star wife, Catherine Zeta Jones, were residents of Bermuda and had met Jim and Lillian at a dinner at the Governor's mansion. They subsequently became friendly and started to visit the island. Few people, it seems, even if they are amongst the biggest movie stars in the world, can resist an invitation to a private island wreathed in so many layers of mystery. Jim, thinking it appropriate for Michael Douglas, decided to rechristen the island 'Gunpowder Island'.

Michael expressed an interest in the film, which was then still in its early stages, and Jim fixed up a theatrical after-dinner screening, projecting the work in progress against a white wall in one of the underground gunpowder vaults.

Michael asked if he could take a copy of the script away. Jim assumed he was simply being polite and that would be the last he would hear on the subject. A few days later, however, the film star rang at 7.30am to say that the script had kept him awake all night. He thought the project was immensely important and wanted to be part of it. A studio was booked and the Michael Douglas narration was completed in a day.

I settled into a seat in the cinema as Jim attempted to make the DVD machine work with the variety of different remote controls that were scattered around the room. None of them, however, were eliciting any sort of response that we could see on the screen. I didn't have a clue where to start with any of them and Jim was becoming irritated. Lillian, as always, came to the rescue. Jim appeared before us on the screen at the helm of a yacht, talking to camera and looking as though he actually knew how to sail.

Films are one of Jim's great passions, so when he heard that James Ivory, one half of the famous Merchant Ivory team, was in need of a backer to finish his latest film his ears pricked up. The meeting between them had come about because Ivory and his writer for fifty years, Ruth Prawer Jhabvala, both had apartments in the same block in New York as Lillian.

'Like most writers,' Jim says, 'Ruth's apartment was littered with eclectic heaps of books and papers, but I noticed that the doors were propped open with Oscars.'

Ivory was in the middle of filming a novel called *The City of Your Final Destination* by Peter Cameron. The bulk of the film had been shot in Uruguay but Ivory had still to shoot scenes in America for the beginning and the end when the financial crisis arrived and he ran out of money. Merchant, who had always taken care of the financial side of the business, had recently died and Ivory seemed somewhat lost in the production jungle.

Jim offered to invest the missing money and half jokingly wondered out loud if he might be able to make a cameo appearance himself, like Alfred Hitchcock famously used to do in his films. Having seen Jim speaking to camera in his own movie, Ivory felt confident to allot him a short speaking part as the mailman who delivers a letter at the beginning of the film. At last he was what his father had wanted him to be.

The atmospheric story centres on a writer arriving at a mysterious, overgrown and beautiful Uruguayan house in the middle of the jungle, hoping to get permission from the eccentric family in residence to write a biography of the former head of the family, a celebrated yet obscure writer. As I read it I couldn't help feeling that I was seeing a faint but eerie reflection of my own situation on Gunpowder Island.

🌐

Few people thought that computers were anything other than 'miracle adding machines' when Jim joined IBM. Thomas J Watson, the founder of the company, actually took IBM out of the computer business at one stage, figuring that electronic calculators were all that people needed. His son, Thomas J Watson Jr, took over in 1952 and the company shipped its first computer. The US Fortune *magazine later described him as the 'most successful capitalist who ever lived'.*

Jim was put to work on a project that the senior management at IBM thought was too fantastical ever really to have a serious market. It was said that even Thomas Watson predicted in 1956 that they would never sell more than twelve of these machines, which meant it probably wasn't worth investing too much time and money in their development, since the company was doing such a roaring business with punch-card machines for containing, sorting and printing data.

Each computer that was manufactured at that time was the size of a large room and Jim's job description was partly to be a boffin in the backroom and partly to be a sales person explaining to corporate customers why these gigantic, expensive machines were the way the world was going to go. During one memorable demonstration in Scotland he electrocuted himself and a picture appeared on the front of the local paper depicting Jim as a typical mad computer scientist with his hair standing on end as the volts shot through him. The headline read 'Miracle Machine Shocks Operator'. On another occasion the weight of the computer was so great it started to bring down the ceiling below, which had to be jacked up by mining experts.

Despite the general level of scepticism about the future usefulness of computers, Jim became an avid believer and a champion for the cause of attaching them to telecommunications, which in the early 1960s still sounded like pure science fiction. He told everyone who would listen that he could envisage a time when computers would all be linked and talking to each other and he wasn't afraid to talk about it and write about it, even though it got him branded as a nut in many quarters. IBM was making enough money to be able to invest in a few crazy ideas and Watson had a growing feeling that there might be something in the proposals that his boffins were putting forward, even if he didn't yet see how they would work.

Fifteen European employees, including Jim, were sent to America for training in computers connected to networks. Jim was then assigned to a ground-breaking teleprocessing project to computerize American Airlines, called SABRE. The system would now seem laughably crude but then seemed unimaginably sophisticated. From there he was sent to the Bank of England and then to Paris to work on similar systems in six European banks.

For Jim it felt like arriving in heaven. Not only was he able to work in a world of scientists and thinkers, striving to change everything about the way the world communicated and did business, but he was also able to indulge his thirst for travel and for exposure to more and varied cultures both in America and Europe.

IBM had created a Systems Research Institute (SRI) in New York, which was a think-tank run along much the same lines as a university except that all the students were employees of the company and extremely highly motivated to learn. The lecturers were also from within the company and tended to be people who the management knew were doing interesting research but who they weren't quite sure how to place in the commercial hierarchy. Like university professors, as well as teaching they were required to be studying something new and different, making themselves world experts on their particular subjects. Jim was invited to go out to New York to join the staff.

He already knew that he loved America. After the stiff formalities and strict social stratas of England, the friendly buzz of New York was a tonic for him. He suddenly found himself able to strike up conversations with the most casual of acquaintances or with people who in England would have left him self-conscious and tongue-tied. Just walking the bustling streets of Manhattan and gazing up at the skyscrapers made him feel charged with a new sort of energy.

'The difference between a London girlfriend and a New York girlfriend', he said, 'was like the difference between a glass of sherry and a dry martini.'

He felt he had arrived in a place where anything might be possible, a million miles from the restrictions of postwar Britain and the self-inflicted limitations of conventional management. For the first time in his life, at the age of twenty-seven, Jim was eating steak and partying at the Waldorf Astoria (although everyone had to drink fruit punch at IBM parties because there was a strict 'no alcohol' policy in the company. When the hotel inadvertently served up pears in wine at an IBM banquet, the company had a bureaucratic meltdown).

The American business community was embracing the idea of computers in a way unlike anything that was happening in Britain. Having fallen in love with the Martini lifestyle of New York, Jim was happy to accept the invitation to join SRI, *even though the thought of lecturing made him deeply nervous and left him shy, sweating, stammering and awkward as he battled to get his audiences to understand what he was talking about and to share his enthusiasms.*

He was right to be nervous because when the feedback came in from the students he did not get good reviews. The comments ranged from 'boring delivery' to 'didn't learn anything'. The management, sensing that they might be trying to force a square peg into a round hole, asked Jim if he would like to change to something else, but by that stage he had become deeply excited by the work going on at SRI and he was determined to develop the highest possible level of communication skills. He could see that if he ever wanted to progress from being a backroom boffin he needed to learn how to be a dynamic speaker. He asked to be given another chance. If he could stay at SRI it meant he could study, travel, write books, teach courses and immerse himself in the problems of systems complexity. It was too good an opportunity to lose, but he understood that his work would all be pointless if he was unable to communicate his discoveries and ideas to other people effectively.

Always being a great believer in teaching yourself the skills you need in life, he deliberately went out to study the speaking techniques of some of the greatest communicators. He watched Laurence Olivier in the theatre, Louis Armstrong in the nightclubs, Dan Rather on television and Billy Graham in the pulpit. He watched the way they held the attention of their audiences, the way they made eye contact, the way they used pauses and changes of volume to bring back anyone whose attention might be wandering. He decided that lecturing could be like acting, something that he had been good at when he was at school. To overcome his shyness he was going to have to create a whole different persona when he was on stage.

Now that he was concentrating on the subject he could see that the best speakers and performers were all following basically the same rules and he worked out how to apply them to his lectures. The next time the students were asked to write assessments the difference was dramatic. They now found Jim an electric speaker, giving comments like 'fascinating', 'held my attention every step of the way' and 'suddenly understood subjects I never thought I would grasp'.

Although he didn't realize the full significance of the change at the time, Jim had mastered the skill that would eventually lead him out of IBM and on to the world stage. What he did realize was that he had discovered a way to excite an audience, and that was a good feeling. He loved controlling them and sensing them filling up with excitement as they took in the ideas he was laying before them. As well as talking within IBM he started to appear in front of larger audiences at industry conferences as a spokesman for the company.

When IBM decided to set up a European version of SRI on the banks of Lake Geneva Jim was asked to be one of the people to go there, set down the guidelines, recruit the staff and lecture.

As well as working on his speaking skills, Jim was also honing his writing skills, submitting a number of technical papers within the company for publication. Out of the blue he was invited to lunch by a man called Karl Karlstrom from a company called Prentice Hall, the world's biggest publisher of textbooks. They met in a little restaurant opposite the United Nations building. Karl was a bearded bloodhound of a man with an unquenchable appetite for Martinis. He had heard about Jim's work from contacts *within IBM and his mission that day was to persuade him to develop some of his papers into books. The two men took an instant liking to one another.*

A few weeks later Jim was sitting in a dingy hotel room in Britain, staring for twenty minutes at a blank sheet of paper before writing the first line of his first book: 'A revolution is happening in the world of data processing.'

He looked down at that one line for the rest of the evening, unable to think of what to say next. The following morning, however, he found that the following few paragraphs had formed in his head during the night and several months later he was able to hand his first manuscript in for publication.

The subjects Jim was writing about were finally catching on. Forward-thinking people all over the world were realizing that something dramatic was happening in the world of technology and they wanted to find out more about it. There weren't many people amongst the boffins and geeks of the early computing world who were able to communicate effectively with the outside world. Jim suddenly found himself in demand. As soon as he finished one book, Karl wanted another, and another, and after a while the royalty cheques started to arrive.

Despite the fact that he had a full-time job, Jim was becoming a writing factory, which involved enormous amounts of work. Even for someone as versed in technology as he was, these were still the pre-word processing days, and he would write everything out on yellow pads in longhand, using Scotch tape and scissors for editing before having the resulting manuscripts typed up.

As ever, Tom Martin was completely bemused by his son's activities.

'But you've written one book,' he protested. 'Why would you want to write another?'

When Jim turned up in Ashby-de-la-Zouche driving a sports car, bought with his royalties, and offered to take his father for a spin with the top down, Tom reluctantly had to admit that maybe the boy was on to something, although his friends down at the British Legion were still wondering out loud, 'When is that lad of yours going to settle down and get a proper job in Ashby?'

Having lived all their lives without luxuries such as cars, fridges, telephones, hot water or indoor plumbing, both Tom and Mabel met all Jim's offers of gifts with looks of puzzlement. Why on earth did he think they needed a fridge when the milk could stand outside on the doorstep? As for a telephone – people might ring the bell in their bedroom in the middle of the night!

In New York word of Jim's ideas was spreading up the company and the day before Christmas Eve in 1965 a call came through from the office of AK Watson, the President of IBM World Trade.

'Mr Watson wants you to brief him on teleprocessing', Jim was informed, 'at his office on First Avenue on December 26th. The meeting will start at nine in the morning and will last all day. There will just be the two of you at the meeting and it is to be kept confidential. No one is to know that it has taken place.'

Jim was due to spend Christmas Day with a girlfriend called Kathy in Toronto, but this was not an instruction that he could even think of turning down. All through Christmas Day, as he watched the family opening their presents, he was planning in his head what he would say the next morning, growing increasingly nervous and excited at the opportunity to influence one of the two most successful men in the business machine industry. Who knew what would happen if he could convert one of the Watsons to his view of the future of computers?

After a big turkey dinner he and Kathy set off to drive the four hundred miles back down to New York that evening. The snow was falling so hard that the airports had all been closed. They were taking it in turns to drive.

At one in the morning, with nightclub music playing softly on the car radio and snow driving into the windscreen, Kathy was at the wheel on the New York Thruway, with Jim lost in thought beside her, when they hit a patch of black ice, careened off the road, through a signpost, down an embankment and into a wall of rock. When they took stock of their situation they realized they were both alive but Jim's face was a mass of blood, having hit the driver's mirror on impact.

The doctors at the hospital that the ambulance took them to wanted him to stay in for observation for a couple of days, but there was no way Jim was going to miss the chance of a one-to-one meeting with AK Watson and he escaped in the small hours of the morning.

The President's aide was waiting for him in the foyer of the First Avenue building as he limped in a few minutes before nine o'clock, bruised and bandaged.

'Do you have flip charts?' the man asked anxiously as he took Jim up in the lift.

'No.' Jim would have smiled if his face hadn't hurt so much. It always struck him as comical that a company that purported to be the most advanced high-technology business in the world relied almost exclusively on flip charts for management communication.

'My god,' the President said as Jim was shown in, 'what the hell happened to you?'

Jim explained and then started to talk about the future of computers and teleprocessing. Over the following few hours the President occasionally interrupted with questions, but on the whole he remained as riveted to the verbal picture Jim was painting of the future as the students at SRI always were.

'A worldwide network of computers?' he said at the end. 'Can IBM really do something like this?'

'In some ways it would be less complicated than the things we are already doing for clients.'

'But it would be so big.'
'Yes, Sir.'
'It means IBM could change the world.'
'Yes, Sir,' Jim replied, making his way towards the door, satisfied that he had managed to get his message across. 'It will fundamentally change the world.'
'OK.' The President slapped him on the back. 'Drive more carefully in future.'

CHAPTER NINE
The Wide View

'I always like to have a beautiful view to look at when I'm thinking,' Jim said as we sat together in the two well-worn armchairs that stood in the largest bay window of his tower, watching the courtship dance of the longtails in the sky over the bright blue ocean.

Once he had discovered that he wrote best early in the mornings, having gone to bed thinking over the problems and possibilities of the future, Jim deliberately sought out places to live where he would be able to sit at his desk and gaze out at far horizons when the sun was coming up.

In London he lived for a while at the top of a house owned by the Redgrave acting dynasty in Chiswick Mall, beside the Thames, with views across the water to Barnes. When he first arrived in America he rented the house of a professor who was going to be out of the country for a while. Only when he arrived at the front door did he discover that it was a mansion standing in twenty-four acres of land on the banks of the mile-wide Hudson River, with its own beach. Every one of the nineteen rooms looked like a magazine illustration.

He later learned that the professor was in a hurry to take a sabbatical somewhere outside the country because he had advised President Kennedy to carry out the ill-advised Bay of Pigs Invasion, and he needed to keep a low profile for a while.

Staying in such beautiful places reawakened in Jim all the longings he had felt as a boy wandering through the gracious, virtually abandoned stately homes around Ashby-de-la-Zouche. If there wasn't a ready-made view, he would conspire to create one. In New York he rented an apartment with a glass room on a high floor projecting out over Madison Avenue in which he started to cultivate orchids in gravel-filled trays of water. The room had views up and down the Avenue and Jim arranged a mirror at a giddying forty-five degrees to reflect the passing traffic below.

When he moved to work for IBM in America full time he bought himself a very old, run-down and picturesque house on a mountain top in Vermont, with two hundred acres of land around it. One of the barns was two hundred years old and had the names of the cows who had lived there painted on the stalls. When Jim saw one of their names was Mabel he felt it was a sign that he was meant to buy it. He immediately set about restoring the house and re-landscaping the grounds, digging lakes and creating natural gardens with the money that was starting to flow in from book royalties. Freshwater ecology fascinated him and he built cascading ponds, including one that was twelve acres in size with a swampy island in the middle. He learned to breed fish and spent hours lost in thought as he studied the habits of birds and otters. He strung hammocks on mountain ledges or by the water's edge – one even spanned a ravine above a waterfall. It was like a giant playground. Although he was still merely an employee at IBM, he was beginning to be able to afford to fulfil some of his childhood fantasies.

At one stage IBM realized that a number of their employees were earning a lot of money by writing books and had a contract drawn up that stated that in future all royalties would go to the company. Horrified, Jim went to his bosses and pointed out that they were basically asking him to choose between his career as an author and his career at IBM. The contract was duly re-written to say that all employees 'apart from James Martin' would pass any royalties they earned to the company. It was beginning to dawn on Jim that he actually did have some value in the marketplace, which gave him some ability to influence his own future.

'What is Sue doing down there?' Jim asked as we sat contemplating the sea view stretched before us.

I peered down at the rocky promontory beyond the beach where I had swum the day before to where Sue appeared to be absorbed with one of Paul's more exotic bench constructions.

'Apparently she's making a photographic record of all Paul's benches around the island,' I explained. 'Lillian has lent her a camera.'

'She should have said,' he said, obviously tickled by the idea. 'She could have borrowed my camera.'

I had a feeling Jim's camera might be something a bit special, having seen the photographs he had taken for the large illustrated book of the island that had been left in our bedroom. It was called *Gunpowder Island: A Bermudian Adventure* and it chronicled the progress of the island from the first day Jim hacked his way on to it with a machete in 1997 through the next five years of feverish clearing, excavating, building and planting. Each stage was illustrated with Jim's own pictures of flowers, fish, trees and views, as well as some of his travel pictures as he went around the world in search of the sculptures and artefacts that now decorated the house and grounds.

The book told the story of the hermit they discovered during the clearing of the undergrowth, living in one room of a ruined cottage, his hair and beard apparently uncut for years. He appeared to live entirely off the fish that he caught around the shores, not bothering to cultivate any fruit or vegetables to supplement his diet. He seemed to have lavish supplies of liquor, which he must have traded for fish. At first he hid from the invaders of his solitude but gradually his confidence grew and he emerged from time to time to regale them with evermore colourful stories. Like Caliban, the monstrous character of *The Tempest*, he was friendly enough when drunk.

'I'll swear upon that bottle to be thy true subject,' Caliban says, 'for the liquor is not earthly ... I'll pluck thee berries; I'll fish for thee, and get thee wood enough ...'

The modern Caliban informed them that he was the boss of the island and inferred that he knew strange things about it.

'Be not afeard,' Caliban says. 'The isle is full of noises, sounds and sweet airs that give delight and hurt not.'

The sight of Sue outside in the sun playing with cameras while we were stuck indoors was eventually too much of a temptation for Jim.

'Let's go for a walk,' he said. 'Have you seen the cottage?'

A few minutes later we were strolling down the heavily overgrown paths to the far end of the island.

'We have more species of plants and flowers here than they have in the Bermuda Botanical Gardens,' Jim said, waving at the planting surrounding us. 'Their experts have been here and can't even identify some of them. There were no palm trees on the island at all when we first arrived. We tried transporting some fully grown ones but they made the boats tip and the roots didn't take well to salt water, so we started growing them ourselves from coconuts. Most of the trees you see now have been grown on the island: fan palms, date palms, bamboo palms that grow to eighty feet ... These' – he pointed to some dark, sculptural-looking plants – 'are cycads and they were on the earth even before the dinosaurs, two hundred million years ago. They can live for anything up to two thousand years.

'We wanted to plant trees that would be stately far in the future, and we wanted to create winding lanes that would become archways of trees. We built these embankments to block the winter gales and covered them in slow-growing tamarisk and Natal plum. In the wind-sheltered areas we planted bougainvillea and flowering trees to provide colour. It will be magnificent long after we are dead.'

I remembered him telling me of how even as a boy he had admired the foresight of gardeners like Capability Brown who had planned landscapes for what they would look like in future centuries.

At the furthest point on the island from the main house there is still the original British army barracks built to house the soldiers guarding the gunpowder, a beautiful ramshackle colonial building that had all but disappeared under the vegetation when Jim rediscovered it. Jim had it renovated to provide extra guest accommodation without losing any of its original character.

A long veranda stretched all the way down one side with tall, shuttered windows surrounded by bougainvillea. Sand had been laid on the ground outside the veranda to provide a boules court to help pass some of the long, leisurely, balmy evenings, and on the other side stood the simple cottage that Jim had had constructed when he first arrived so that he could live on the island while the more complicated main house was still being planned and built.

'I hired a man called Hartley Watlington,' Jim said as he forced open a door that had warped shut from the sea air and led me into the cottage. 'He's an expert in Bermuda cottages and built this to look like it had been here since 1850, to blend in with the barracks.'

We came through a kitchen into a central room with a large open fireplace. Jim seemed to be lost in memories as he looked around.

'It would be very cosy in here on an evening with a roaring fire banked up, burning our way through the timber that was being cleared from all over the island. David Bowie and Iman came over here for supper a few times.'

For a moment I wasn't sure that I had heard right. 'David Bowie and Iman came here for supper?'

'Oh, yes,' Jim smiled absent mindedly. 'It was at the time when he was planning to go on to the internet in a big way, just before the dotcom bubble burst. He wanted to know if it was possible to sell fine art over the net. I told him I was sure it was and he came over to talk about it. They lived on Bermuda at the time too, so we went to their place as well. Iman is stunningly beautiful.'

He appeared wistful for a moment. Thinking about beautiful women often seems to make Jim look rather wistful.

🌐

Jim met Charity Howland Anders in New York in 1969 and was immediately smitten. He was thirty-six and despite having had a number of girlfriends he had been too immersed in his work and his dreams to settle down properly into a relationship. Charity was only twenty-five, stunning, eccentric, intelligent and vibrantly alive. In Manhattan taxis she liked to stick her nose out the window like a dog in order to feel the wind in her hair.

Charity was a direct descendent of John Howland, one of the original pilgrims who arrived in America on the Mayflower *in 1620, and the only one who fell overboard and had to be rescued. He married Elizabeth Tilley, another pilgrim, so Charity was one of the few people descended from two of the founders.*

Her family lived in a totally isolated place in Virginia twenty miles from the nearest shop, but on a beautiful wide river. Her father was a tyre salesman from New York who had somehow managed to get a schooner and become a member of the New York Yacht Club before suddenly giving it all up and moving to the middle of nowhere with no explanation.

By that stage Jim was enjoying his bachelor life and even though he had fallen deeply in love he was nervous about giving up his freedom. Charity, however, wanted to get married and her father was putting on the pressure. A wedding needed to be organized and Jim wasn't sure quite where to start. To add to the complications Tom and Mabel would not make a trip to America and Charity's father would not travel to England. Finally swept up in the excitement of this new adventure, Jim decided to take the plunge and suggested they choose a neutral venue. In 1971 they married at dawn in a tiny white chapel on a hill on Virgin Gorda in the Virgin Islands with the Atlantic on one side, the Caribbean on the other and a three-hundred-and-sixty-degree view. They held the wedding breakfast on a beach called The Baths, which was a mass of exotic pools and grottos formed from boulders with the sea crashing over them. Charity's parents came and the bride wore a white wedding dress with a long veil that billowed in the wind as they exchanged their vows.

'Of course, they got married at dawn,' Jim's grandfather in England, who was well into his nineties by then, muttered when told the news. 'Only the right thing to do. Everyone used to do it. That's why they call it the "wedding breakfast".'

In the same year Jim was summoned to Washington. A long black government limousine picked him up from his hotel and hummed quietly across town to the State Department building, where he was to be briefed on how to conduct himself on an exchange mission to Moscow. It was the height of the Cold War.

The idea had been dreamed up by the people at the Ford Foundation who believed it would be beneficial for a dozen independent computer experts to meet with a dozen top

Soviet ones to explore areas where there might be a fruitful exchange of information or cooperative research. The Foundation had originally been set up by two members of the Ford family to provide grants for the promotion of peace, freedom and education throughout the world. It is still going today and in 2008 reported assets of $11 billion.

The State Department was nervous that the naïve scientists would be lured into traps by wily communists and would open themselves up to blackmail, so they were rigorously briefed on the relevant etiquette and the dangers of drinking too much vodka and ending up in compromising situations.

'If you return to your hotel room and find a naked woman lying in the bed,' a straight faced official told them, 'you must close the door and contact the American Embassy immediately.'

More long black limousines awaited them in Moscow and carried them to a welcome cocktail party. As shy as always, Jim was standing in the corner of the room, cautiously nursing a soda and surveying the crowd, when one of the Russian scientists came over.

'Hello,' he said without the trace of an accent, 'my name is ******.'

It turned out the man had been to Oxford and they chatted amiably about every subject under the sun.

The following day the meetings started. The Russians were shockingly backward in their uses of technology, but thought the Americans were shockingly backward in their use of mathematics. During informal conversations, lubricated by lavish quantities of vodka, they discovered that their hosts were particularly good at things like the computations needed for the space programme. They were also highly sophisticated at economic forecasting, which was particularly complex in a totalitarian state of that size.

The second meeting was in Turin, with KGB agents following the Russians wherever they went to ensure that they didn't try to defect. Both sides were surprised by how much they liked one another once they had broken through the language barrier and openly wondered why their leaders were putting so much money and effort into building weapons to try to destroy one another. Relationships were forming between the two sides and the Russians expressed puzzlement as to why an Englishman like Jim would actually choose to live in America, which they had been told was such a terrible place. Jim tried to convince them that they had been misinformed about the US and even sent them photographs once he got home, but he never heard back, so had no idea if the pictures were ever allowed to reach their destination.

The man called ****** presented a paper on process control, but when asked questions it was obvious to Jim and the Americans that he knew little about his chosen subject. They became convinced that he could not have written the paper himself and voiced their suspicions to the State Department officials. Investigations revealed that he was indeed not a scientist as he was pretending, but was a member of the intelligence organization in Moscow that spent its time watching the US.

Two years later the Director of SRI in New York summoned Jim into his office and told him that there was a Soviet scientist visiting the States and that the Institute had been asked by the State Department to entertain him and show him a few things.

'Would you mind hosting the guy around New York, Jim? Since you have experience with the Ruskies.'

'Of course,' Jim said, and the Director handed him a dossier on the visitor. He opened the first page and saw a photograph of ******.

'This man is not a computer scientist,' Jim said. 'He's a spy.'

'For God's sake, Martin. You watch too many James Bond films.' The Director shook his head. 'He can't be a

spy. Look, I've got a list of the installations he has visited already. They wouldn't have let him in if he was an intelligence agent.'

Jim perused the list and handed it back. 'If I were a Russian intelligence agent those are exactly the installations I would want to see.'

A few hours later he was called back to the Director's office.

'The powers that be still want you to act as ******'s host, but they have made up a list of things you can and can't show him and things you can and can't talk about.'

Jim did as he was told.

CHAPTER TEN
The Fortune Makers

As we walked back along the other side of the island, Jim paused at one of Paul's seats in an area that had been laid out as an Italian garden but was already disappearing under the weight of its own vegetation. His eyes focused on the white boats bobbing on the water and the brightly coloured mansions on the other side with their immaculate lawns reaching down to the shore.

'A lot of people spend the early parts of their life working to make as much money as possible,' he said after a while. 'I certainly did. But then you get to a stage where you have all you need. Maybe because you have sold up a company that you started, or you have merely built a large pile of capital. Most of the people over there have massive sums of money just sitting in shares or in bank accounts. What we need to convince them of is that they will have much more fun if they use that money to invest in creating something wonderful than if they just spend their time drifting around in boats or on golf courses. Ideally, of course, I would like them to put their spare money into The 21st Century School because the more funding we have the more we can achieve, but there are plenty of other things that they could be investing in, which would help to move humankind towards a better future.

'It's not philanthropy. I get quite annoyed when I hear myself described as a philanthropist. I'm actually quite mean. Just ask Lillian or Duncan. I want to create something

I really believe in. That means investing in great people. It is actually in all our interests to invest in the future, but we have to do it in the right way. It is all about harnessing "idea power".

'Bill Gates is an interesting case in point. He came to visit me in Bermuda in about 1985 when his fortune was over $10 billion and Microsoft was already a major force in the marketplace. He flew in economy class, wearing really scruffy clothes. On the immigration form he described his occupation as "programmer". Corinthia's nanny put a bumper sticker on her car saying "If you're rich, I'm single." He was almost a caricature of a nerd who rocked backwards and forwards in his chair all the time. He didn't want to go to a good restaurant. "You have to eat," he said, "it's a basic bodily function, so let's get it over with as quickly as possible – like going to the men's room." It was obvious he had absolutely no idea what the social consequences of the computer revolution would be, but he sat up long into the night, like an excited child, discussing software strategy. He had almost no social skills, but it was clear that he was creating something amazing. It was only after he married Melinda, nine years later, that the idea of using his money to do something socially constructive came about.'

Jim fell quiet for a moment and we both watched a million-dollar schooner sliding past.

'Some people question whether I am doing the best thing by putting my money into an academic organization like Oxford, which gives the impression of already being well heeled. Would I do better to fund a healthcare scheme somewhere in the developing world? But The 21st Century School has extraordinary leverage – it has two hundred or more of the world's best minds working on the world's most difficult problems. We need to ensure that the best thinking possible goes into our transition to the future. If we rush into curing short-term problems piecemeal we might achieve dramatic and short-term results, but spoil a wider approach that would work better in the long run.

'One of the biggest problems on the planet, for instance, is population growth. We are currently approaching seven billion people in the world – it'll go to nine billion. There were around two billion when I was a boy. Sir Crispin Tickell at the school pointed out the other day that if that happened with caterpillars, or kangaroos, or hippopotamuses, we'd be scared stupid, but because it's us we think it's OK. I was in India recently and it had been thirty-seven years since my first visit. During that time the population had grown by six hundred and thirty million. Years ago, I stayed with a government minister who for a long time was the Minister for Population Control. He was a charming, white-haired, articulate man and we sat up late into the night and he explained Hindu philosophy to me. "You know," he said jovially in the early hours of the morning, "I must have been the most unsuccessful executive of all time."'

Jim chuckled at the memory

'The growth is largely due to the fact that everyone is living longer thanks to better healthcare. We lowered the death rate but didn't lower the birth rate. Diseases that used to carry off a large proportion of the children born in poverty have been eradicated in many parts of the world. And we can always take that process further if we choose. We could, for instance, put all our efforts into eradicating malaria – initially by giving out free mosquito nets. In the short term that is a very desirable goal. But if all the people who would have died from malaria live to an age where they can have children, you have increased the stresses and strains on resources in the poorest parts of the world.

'It is an enormous moral and ethical problem and we need to do all we can to ensure that the greatest brains in the world are not only working effectively in their individual areas of expertise, but that they are also communicating with one another so that their ideas can be cross fertilized and integrated. It is no good curing one problem if the result is a hundred new problems somewhere else. That is why I think that organizations like The 21st Century School are so important and why they need to be continually cross-pollinating ideas.'

As we strolled back up the house through the gardens we gazed across the turquoise water at shoals of small flying fish being chased by larger ones.

'I have a theory', he said, 'that when it comes to deciding on goals in life there are three types of people. The first type spends their lives seeking happiness. The second type spends their lives striving to make money. The third type spends their lives trying to be creative, inventing things, making films or doing something constructive. The third group usually achieves happiness. The second group sometimes finds happiness but only because in order to make money they often have to do something constructive and interesting. But the ones who spend their whole lives seeking happiness find it as elusive as quicksilver.'

He paused for a moment, as if checking if he still agreed with his own theory, before giving a short nod of satisfaction and walking on in the hope of finding some lunch in the house.

Following his success working on teleprocessing systems for American Airlines and Pan Am, Jim was sent back to London to work on a worldwide system for British Airways (then called BOAC). The salesman who was working on the account (who later became a close advisor to Margaret Thatcher) was failing to win the order so IBM took him off the job and asked Jim to handle the account.

His enthusiasm must have carried the day because he won the $10 million order, which was the largest IBM World Trade had ever had at that time. To show their appreciation *the company gave him an outstanding contribution award of $500. He immediately worked out how much more he would have got if he had been working on a five-per cent commission. Not for the first time, it occurred to him that whereas the employers of the nineteenth century grew rich on the physical sweat of their employees, their twentieth-century equivalents were running intellectual sweatshops in much the same way, paying people a tiny percentage of what they could earn for themselves on the open market.*

By the 1970s IBM was one of the greatest corporate success stories for half a century. There were times when IBM posted among the largest profits of any industrial corporation in history. Thomas J Watson's chauffer, from Sweden, invested $1,000 in IBM shares and they were worth $8 million by the time Watson stepped down and the chauffer retired.

However, the US government brought the biggest antitrust case in history against the company, which resulted in the largest trial of its sort ever. IBM's management became in thrall to lawyers, who produced a staggering thirty million pages of printed documentation in IBM's defence. The court case went on for five US presidencies (Johnson, Nixon, Ford, Carter and Reagan), and the outcome was one page from the government with only one sentence: 'This case has no merit.'

Despite his continued success within the company, Jim was becoming increasingly disillusioned with the bureaucracy that had grown up during the reign of the lawyers. So when an old friend of his, John Collins, suggested they should organize public seminars at which Jim would lecture, he was willing to give it some serious thought. John had also been to Oxford, at Wadham College next door to Keble, and was now a brilliant, shaggy professor of computer science at Lancaster University. His idea was that he would do all the organization and administration, while Jim would be the star attraction.

The management at IBM liked the idea but their lawyers said that employees could only lecture for non-profit organizations. John's answer was simple: he created a non-profit organization.

Taking all the skills that he had built up during his time as a lecturer at SRI, and drawing on his enormous experience at installing systems inside major blue-chip organizations, Jim put together a seminar and John went out to sell it. The first event was a success and word spread so that the audience had swelled dramatically by the second one.

Anxious to give the best talks possible, Jim wanted to speak about the whole field of computer science, but IBM became uncomfortable at the thought of him talking about products from rival companies. The lawyers then grew nervous about all the confidential corporate material that Jim had access to. At one seminar in Paris, at a time when IBM was spending around a billion dollars trying to build a highly secret new line of computers called Future Systems, a reporter who attended the seminar wrote about the system as if he had heard Jim talking about it. The lawyers at IBM were incensed and called every one of the two hundred delegates by transatlantic phone to ask them if Jim had mentioned Future Systems, recording every call so that it could be used in evidence against him. Every delegate told the same story –, that Jim had not mentioned confidential systems – but the lawyers insisted on censoring all Jim's books and lectures from that point on.

Despite the fact that he was making a great deal of money, Jim was finding this a harder and harder atmosphere in which to work. He was becoming increasingly intrigued by the individuals who were starting to become millionaires in the computing field. He could see that all of them had shares in the companies they were setting up. The great fortunes of the 1980s were still unheard of but Jim could see that the rapid future growth of technology that he anticipated would present some stunning financial opportu-

nities. To make really big money, he decided, one had to be in at the start of a successful company. All these thoughts were already brewing at the back of his mind when he received a call from a man called Barry Yampol.

'I've read your book Future Developments in Telecommunications,*' Barry said. 'I have an idea for a new corporation. Can I come and talk to you?'*

Jim's opening words in the preface of that book were 'A handful of entrepreneurs have become telecommunications millionaires. More will follow.'

Yampol was the President of Graphic Scanning, a company using existing telecommunications links to provide new services. He and Jim put together a business plan and launched Graphnet Systems Inc, which was to use computers to relay facsimile messages, transmitting them from computers, telegraph machines, data terminals and fax machines. It all sounds quaintly old fashioned now but at the time it was groundbreaking. Because they didn't think it was an industry that they would want to be in, IBM gave permission for Jim to be chairman and co-founder of Graphnet. As the whole sector took off, however, they realized their mistake and Jim was informed that there was now a conflict of interest. He would have to sell his shares and resign his chairmanship.

Jim was forced to comply, but as he watched Graphnet grow into a large company and the shares soar in value he began to question whether he was right to stay with IBM for much longer, since they seemed to be cramping his style at every turn. At the same time he was unsure if he could survive for long at the cutting edge of the industry without access to all the information that his position at SRI afforded him. To leave IBM and take his chances in the world as a freelancer would require considerable courage and a lot of thought.

CHAPTER ELEVEN

Shooting Stars and Northern Lights

'Look at this,' Lillian said as we came into the house. 'It's extraordinary.' She swung her laptop around on the table for us to see. It was startling to see a familiar lineup of celebrity jury members led by Simon Cowell. Was Lillian really a follower of *Britain's Got Talent*?

'Someone told me about it this morning,' she explained, obviously seeing my surprise. 'Apparently it's had about twenty million hits already on YouTube and the numbers are growing all the time.'

We watched as Susan Boyle, the epitome of the fabled ugly duckling, strode out on to stage and we listened as she was gently mocked and patronized by the sneering judges and live audience, only to shock her tormentors into stunned and reverent silence a few moments later with the beauty and confidence of her singing voice. It was a perfect fairytale moment, which was doubtless why so many tens of millions of people were diving in to watch it and recommending others to do the same – even people like us on a tiny island in the middle of the second mightiest ocean on the planet. Within a few weeks the number of viewings would be approaching two hundred million.

'This is the sort of thing that will be the death of intelligent Hollywood,' Jim said a few minutes later, once the singing was over and the 'happy ending' to the little story had been viewed.

'How can they hope to sell the world intelligent, thoughtful movies that require viewers to buy tickets and concentrate for a couple of hours when millions would rather get a quick emotional hit like this without having to pay for it? But it also shows how massive the power of networks like the internet can be. It's feasible that once the whole world is connected, an item like this could be seen by most people on the planet within a few hours.

'Marshall McLuhan said "the Medium is the Message", but that's an exaggeration. What he meant was that the medium changes the message. You can say different things in a book than you can say on television. Live lectures can be more powerful than video, but video can say things that live lectures cannot. Hyperdocuments enable their user to navigate through vast bodies of information, with expert systems built into them. Multimedia presentations can be very powerful if the human presenter remains in control.

'Too often today the medium swamps the message. Television is dominated by television professionals; the cinema is dominated by cinematographers who will spend $100 million on a movie and a $100,000 on the script. You can see how well people respond when a genuinely interesting or moving moment rises up.' He gestured towards the screen. 'Everyone immediately tells everyone else about it and word spreads at an ever increasing speed.

'I was filmed a few years ago at the Smithsonian for a spectacular video wall consisting of twelve screens. It was a masterpiece of cinematography and preposterously expensive, shot with seventy-millimetre film. But it said nothing worth saying. When I took Corinthia to see it the only comment she made at the end was that I should have used hairspray. For a valuable transfer of knowledge, the master of the subject must dominate the communication process, not the master of cinematography.

'A great communicator knows the capabilities of different media and can select the medium most effective for the communication required. YouTube here, drawing on the raw material of television, is the perfect medium for communicating this moment with Susan Boyle. Nothing else could have achieved that, but this is just the beginning. The reproduction of the clip we've just watched is not that brilliant. It's the equivalent, maybe, to some of the early colour television broadcasts in the 1960s. That will soon be changed. High-bandwidth networks for high-definition wall screens will change the way we watch and shop and everything else. Many people will have home theatres better than a movie theatre.

'So much of what we see on television is mind-shatteringly boring, with techniques left over from earlier times. Mainstream television news is already pointless for everything beyond bullet-point headlines because the broadcasters have so little time to devote to every subject that they are trying to cover. Video internet news, on the other hand, allows you to explore.

'When that pilot was bringing his plane down into the Hudson River after a flock of geese destroyed both engines, you could follow the whole ten-minute conversation between him and the control tower on the internet. It was fantastically exciting. But on the network news you got only a few minutes of coverage with lots of pointless interviews with onlookers who had nothing interesting to say beyond the fact that they had seen it happen.'

So much of the world we live in today is just as Jim predicted it would be in books he published forty or more years ago. It is hard to imagine now what a leap of imagination it would have taken for AK Watson in 1965 to understand how in 2009 a woman like Susan Boyle could have become virtually a household name all over the world within just a few hours. At that stage the world was only just getting used to the movies of Elvis Presley.

It was November 1977. The autumn leaves of Vermont had fallen, leaving the trees stark and dramatic. The locals call it 'the stick season'. Jim and Charity were having a weekend house party and one of the guests was John Collins, who had organized Jim's first independent seminars. John was with his new wife, Margot, a former pig farmer from the north of England. Margot had given up smoking cigarettes and was chain-smoking cigarillos instead.

Jim and Charity's daughter, Corinthia, was just over a year old and her godfather, the South African poet and son of the Bishop of Zululand Leo Aylen, who Jim had met when he was living in New York, was also staying for the weekend.

Charity had cooked a roast dinner and the group was sitting around the fire afterwards feeling mellow. The valley outside, which belonged to the house, was silent and black beyond the windows. John was attempting to persuade Jim to take a year's leave from IBM to try something radically different. He was suggesting that he himself would also take a year's sabbatical from his university and they would both travel the world with Charity and Margot, and Corinthia, staging more seminars like the ones they had been experimenting with, to see if they could make some serious money.

'At the end of the year we can decide if we want to go back to our jobs at IBM and Lancaster,' John said, 'or if we will stay permanently on the road.'

Both men were finding the restrictions of their current jobs irksome and this seemed like a good way to test the waters of self-employment. Jim would select the subject matter for the seminars, design the programme and do the lecturing while John would do the marketing, plan the finances and decide on the venues.

'We could do six seminars in the year,' he explained, 'two in America maybe, then one in England, France, Germany

and Australia. Maybe we could come back and do a final one in the US if things were going well.'

John was brimming with enthusiasm, having been hatching the plans for some time. Jim and the two wives were treading more cautiously as they tried to assess the potential risks of taking such a big step. But as the bottle of Scotch was emptied everyone began to believe that they could be on to something good.

The women eventually went to bed at around midnight but the men kept talking, too excited now to sleep. John started scribbling down wild financial estimates, Jim talked about the messages he wanted to get across about future technology, and Leo, being a poet, talked about the meaning of life.

By two in the morning the Scotch had done its work and John and Jim shook hands on the deal. If it worked John would leave the university and Jim would leave IBM for good. If it didn't work at least they would have had a great adventure.

'From now on', John said, 'you'll be "James Martin", no more "Jim" or "Jimbo". It's all about market image. And no middle initials either. Whoever heard of "James F Bond"?'

Needing some fresh air, they went outside to find the entire night sky – a hundred and eighty degrees – ablaze with the cascading waterfall of colour that is the Northern Lights or Aurora Borealis, the most science fiction-like sight you can see. It seemed like a sign from the heavens and the men walked until dawn along the mountain's dirt roads through bare-branched trees, looking up at the celestial fireworks display. There were no other lights, no signs of human habitation in any direction. It felt to Jim like they were on top of the world, balanced on the edge of the universe.

IBM agreed to give Jim the year off and John organized the first seminar to run for three days in a small hotel on the shores of Lake Windermere in England. There were sixty attendees, which was the maximum the hotel could hold. Jim talked solidly for the whole three days and the reaction of all the delegates at the end was entirely positive. It seemed the moment was finally right for the outside world to begin to listen to the messages that Jim wanted to get across. Within a few months John was able to fill venues with two or three hundred senior managers in a variety of countries, charging them several thousand dollars a head for the privilege of hearing Jim speak.

By the end of the year Jim realized he had made a million dollars from the venture, which was more than any of the senior managers at IBM were making at the time. John had proved his point. It was time to go freelance.

The senior executive at IBM gave what was obviously meant to be a reassuring smile when Jim handed in his notice.

'We understand you have been having some problems,' he said, which was the first Jim had heard about it. 'A mid-life crisis can happen to anyone, Jim. Let's discuss your personal goals. We want you to know that we won't hold this against you in any way.'

'What do you mean?' Jim asked, puzzled. 'I'm leaving the company.'

The other man shook his head sympathetically and continued to work through his armoury of techniques for persuading misguided employees not to hand in their notice, issuing dire warnings of how hard life could be 'outside the company'. It reminded Jim of the techniques the British government officials had used on him when he had declined to work on the hydrogen bomb during his National Service. Eventually the executive was forced to accept that Jim was serious. He was going to take the plunge.

That year Jim wrote his thirteenth book, The Wired Society, *which was later nominated for a Pulitzer Prize. The world had still not seen personal computers, mobile phones or Blackberries. There were no digital cameras, world-wide web or ATM machines. There was no e-mail, and no companies like Amazon or eBay had been dreamed up, but Jim was predicting all of them. He believed that all these developments were inevitable because of the growth of the numbers of transistors on a chip, the growth of small memory devices, the deployment of cellular wireless technology and packet-switching and the steady increase in telecommunications bandwidth. He predicted that by the year 2000 we would see 'a networked planet'. More and more people were beginning to realize that he knew what he was talking about and wanted the chance to listen to what he had to say.*

CHAPTER TWELVE
Sailing

Duncan had been promising to prepare his yacht so that we could go out sailing since the day we had arrived. Boating, it seems, is the lifeblood of most of the inhabitants of Bermuda. Lillian was keen for us to have a change of scene before we came down with 'island fever', but Jim wanted to have some time alone in his tower. Another couple were recruited to join the party.

'You'll enjoy them,' Jim chuckled before disappearing up his staircase. 'He's a wine master and she used to be a showgirl and model in Holland. She trained tigers. She's obsessed with them, always wearing a tiger's tooth in her ear. She's over six feet tall.'

Jim still takes the same delight in eccentric individuals as he did when he first bicycled away from his parents' house, and when he arrived at Oxford and saw how multi-coloured the world outside Ashby-de-la-Zouche could be.

It's easy to see why Duncan stayed on as manager of the island once his main work as the project's architect was finished. In fact it is hard to imagine how anyone could bring themselves to leave such a pleasant life. The house, which he shares with his partner, Helen, who works as a lawyer in Hamilton, stands on the dock next to a newly designed boathouse. It is the sort of open-plan, bohemian cottage that most of us only ever get to stay in on holidays, and Duncan's boat bobs at the jetty no more than ten paces from the front door, or anchors peacefully a hundred meters from the shore.

Most keen sailors have to fit their hobby around inflexible working hours and then have to travel many miles from their homes and their offices to wherever they can find moorings for their beloved boats. At every stage the costs and stresses soar and the amount of time actually spent messing about on the craft has to be severely limited. Duncan has none of that. As Jim says, for a life of eco-affluence you first have to 'work out what it is that you enjoy doing most'.

It was a perfect afternoon with just enough breeze to give us an exhilarating turn of speed, but not enough to alarm two people who were total novices at sailing. We swept along the coast past the waterfront in Hamilton and on round the bay. Small children bobbed past, learning the ropes in what looked like little more than toy boats. The sea and the sky were an unreal shade of blue and the breeze was warm as we tacked round and headed back towards Gunpowder Island, where I knew Jim would be in the tower and might very well be watching us at that moment.

Passing boats provided a constantly changing but soothing landscape from every window in the house. Once or twice a day mighty cargo ships or cruise liners would slip past the island, the top decks almost on a level with Jim's tower window, tourists watching the house just as the inhabitants of the house would be watching them, wondering no doubt what it must feel like to live in such an apparently perfect place.

'All that fuss the planners made about it looking too stark when you first built it,' one of the other sailors scoffed to Duncan, 'but look at the way it's blended in now the trees have grown.'

'You must feel very proud every time you look at it from out here,' I suggested, knowing that he had deliberately designed the island to make the buildings blend with nature, wanting it to look as if they had always been there, seeming to grow out of the nature surrounding them.

Duncan smiled self-deprecatingly. 'The trouble is,' he said, 'I keep seeing new things I'd like to do. I keep having new ideas.'

Most newly built houses start with an overview that becomes a design that is established and finalized before construction starts. With Gunpowder Island there had been no such process, which was partly why the result was so magical. When Jim first bought the island he had no idea that he and Duncan would find eight quarries, or that he would uncover stone ruins, tunnels, old steam engines, shafts, towers, hidden paths, steps and secret gardens, or twelve thousand square feet of underground gunpowder vaults. Many of their plans had to change and adapt as every day they discovered new wonders beneath the undergrowth and gained experience, learning from trial and error what would work and what would not, what plants would grow and thrive and what would shrivel and die. The result had been an evolution, albeit a fairly fast one. Computers make this sort of evolutionary design possible because you can start with a plan but easily modify it as new ideas are born and new lessons learned. The problem is that planning authorities still live in the nineteenth century.

'The island looks nothing like the first plan we had,' Jim had told me that morning. 'It was a bit like a start-up company with a business plan that has to keep changing and adapting at "internet speed". It's the way everything will have to work in future and it is making the world a much more exciting place to live in. You can see the changes reflected in the trouble that some of the world's biggest companies are in, like the motor industry giants. Sooner or later they have got to accept that they have to adapt fast to the changing environment or they will die, just as they had to adapt from building horse-drawn carriages a hundred years ago.'

At a moment like that, speeding across bright blue waters on the wind, it was hard to remember quite why we are all so enslaved to the motor car for our survival. It suddenly seemed obvious that things are going to have to change sooner regarding the wasteful and destructive petrol engine rather than later, and The 21st Century School has an institute dedicated to studying the car of the future.

'There are four main non-petrol power sources that are being researched at the moment,' Jim had explained. 'There are batteries, which are getting better all the time. There are high-power capacitors that take a big charge whenever the car brakes, which save lots of power. Then there are fuel cells, which are like batteries but use chemicals that you add to rather than charge. Hydrogen is beautiful for cars because you could have a container the size of a large briefcase, which the supermarket could fill up for you, and it is the lightest element on earth. But at the moment we need coal power stations to generate hydrogen, so we have to find an alternative to that. We could do it with wind and solar but I think it would be better to use a benign form of nuclear power.

'We could get rid of petrol engines today if we had the political will, but there are still far too many vested interests at the moment. It would be relatively easy on an island the size of Bermuda to say that petrol engines will be banned in five years' time, but if you tried to do that in the US or Europe the vested interests would lose a fortune. In truth we should stop subsidizing the petroleum car industry because then it would quickly fade away due to market forces and we would have to come up with alternatives more quickly than is otherwise going to happen.'

I pondered his words as we sped on past the waterside mansions of people who must, on the whole, make up a fair percentage of the 'vested interests' Jim was talking about.

A freelance writer and lecturer can live anywhere he or she likes in the world, and once he had left IBM Jim, with all the rigour of a systems analyst, set about choosing a new home base. He knew he was going to be travelling a lot, particularly between America and Europe, and he also knew it would be nice to be somewhere with a pleasant climate whenever he was resting or writing. He was also unsure how long the money would keep rolling in for and was therefore anxious to avoid any country that would tax him too highly on his first few years of earnings. Bermuda, with its beautiful beaches, kept coming up as the best possible option.

The only ripple on this otherwise tranquil pond was that the Governor of Bermuda, Sir Richard Sharples, had been assassinated in 1973 while out walking his dog. The two culprits, who happened to be black, were hanged for the crime. This had led to terrifying riots, and luxury real estate plunged in price.

Jim was pretty sure that the trouble was a momentary blip in Bermuda's peaceful history and he found that properties in Tucker's Town, which would previously have been out of his price range, were now half their normal price.

Tuppenny House was a white stone expansion of an older property known as Ha'penny House, which was believed to have been the haunt of theatrical luminaries like Noel Coward and Gertrude Lawrence. The gardens sloped down to one private beach and the house had access to another on the other side of a narrow peninsula. When it was windy on one side it was always calm on the other. The house was built on land owned by the famous Mid-Ocean Golf Club, the scene of war talks between Churchill and Roosevelt, which meant Jim was obliged to join the club even though he had no intention of ever playing even a single round of golf.

Since the money took a while to start flowing in from the seminars, Jim had to start by letting the house out whenever he was travelling. Watching The Johnny Carson Show *one night he heard the controversial black comedian Richard Pryor talking about a house he had rented from 'some computer nut in Tucker's Town' and realized the comedian was talking about him.*

'It's always hard to decide where to go on holiday, you know,' Pryor was telling his host. 'If you go to Acapulco they tear the shirt off your back because they all recognize you, but in Tucker's Town I was recognized for my true status in life – slave!'

John and Jim ended up doing eight seminars in their first year and sixteen in 1979. A year later the number had grown to twenty, grossing $8 million in a year. They would have one guest speaker for ninety minutes in each seminar but otherwise Jim lectured for the whole five days. He used no notes, always talking off the top of his head.

Offstage he never lost his shyness, but onstage he grew increasingly confident of his ability to hold people's attention and give them what they wanted. He found that he would go through an 'elevator transformation' each day. At the top of the hotel elevator Charity would grab him, stare into his eyes and say 'Showtime!' and by the time he walked out at the bottom he was ready to perform. He had no one to understudy him and so he knew he always had to turn up once he was booked. He could never allow bad weather or ill health to delay him. He must never be late, never be jet-lagged, never be performing below par. Over the coming years he found himself lecturing with flu, migraine, Delhi belly and broken ribs. Once on stage he would find that the rush of adrenaline would sweep aside any pains or symptoms he might have otherwise had.

Companies in the Third World were as anxious to hear how to build computer systems for the future as their counter-

parts in the First World, so John arranged for Jim to speak in countries like India as well. They couldn't possibly charge the same sort of fees, but the audiences could be double the normal size. One of India's glossiest computer magazines dedicated an entire eighty-two-page issue to Jim, calling him 'The Modern-Day Prophet'.

As soon as he could afford to do some work to Tuppenny House, Jim built a new wing and a first-floor office for himself with a glass wall looking out over the ocean. During the first year of freedom he, Charity and Corinthia travelled together, excited by every new country and city they came to. Often they would throw parties during the seminars and Corinthia would career happily around among the adults, watched proudly by her parents. Like Jim, Charity was an only child. She shared his belief that there were definite benefits to having no siblings and they didn't intend to have any more children.

Many of the biggest names in the business world wanted to pick Jim's brains, all of them desperate to understand what was happening in their own companies and how they might be able to prepare themselves better for whatever the future might hold. If he protested that he was too busy they would merely send their private jets for him, or fly into Bermuda themselves. When Kerry Packer, then Australia's richest man with a net worth of about $6 billion, asked to see him, Jim was happy to go for the afternoon.

'So,' the legendary media tycoon growled, 'convince me if you can how technology is going to affect my businesses.'

Jim talked for three hours about the coming of the internet and how it would eventually erode the revenues of traditional newspapers. He discussed hypertext and satellites, optical transmission, cellular radio and the impact of globalism on business. Eventually Packer held up a giant hand to stop him. After what seemed to Jim like an age he stood up, leaned his enormous, athletic frame on the desk, pushed his craggy, bronzed face close to Jim's and bellowed, 'You make me feel old!', slamming the door as he walked out.

As well as the business community, many political world leaders have summoned Jim over the years, hoping to be able to understand better what is going to happen next.

On the JP Morgan Advisory Board Jim met Lee Kuan Yew, the founder of modern Singapore, who remained in power for over thirty years and who Jim describes as 'a common-sense genius'.

'He received a lot of bad press in the West when he was in power because he was authoritarian,' Jim says, 'having zero tolerance for drugs and forbidding people from chewing gum or spitting in the street. But without him Singapore could easily have remained a Third World country instead of becoming the economic powerhouse it is today, as well as being a clean, green city that is a pleasure to live in, although some of the original character has been destroyed.'

During the 1980s Jim met both Reagan and Thatcher. Knowing that he was going to be meeting the Iron Lady he had prepared a very concise message. 'It's absolutely vital that you break up British Telecommunications,' he told her as she looked at him intently, 'as America has done. If not it will severely damage your goals.'

She was listening and put him in touch with Sir Keith Joseph, who was at the time credited as being the 'power behind the throne' of Thatcherism and was then Secretary of State for Industry. Jim spent many hours talking to the Secretary at his home in Chelsea over the following months. Every time he paused to ensure that his audience was still following him, Sir Keith would say, 'What else can you tell me?' and Jim would start talking again.

A few weeks after their final meeting, while at a seminar in Paris, Jim received a call asking if he would be willing to become a government advisor. He politely declined. The thought of trying to do battle with the British civil service and drag them towards the twenty-first century kicking and screaming did not seem as attractive as the life he was currently living. He'd had a similar offer in America at the beginning of the 1970s, while he was still at IBM, when he was offered the job of Assistant Secretary of Defense for Telecommunications. Intrigued by the offer, Jim stalled for time, but the department was becoming impatient and wanted him to go to Washington immediately.

'I can't come right away,' Jim replied, 'I'm about to go to Switzerland to give a seminar.'

'Don't worry, we'll get you to Switzerland in time, on our planes if necessary.'

Jim continued to prevaricate, knowing that if he accepted this tempting offer he would never be able to return to IBM in case of accusations of conflicts of interest.

'Mr Martin,' the voice from Washington was grave, 'there comes a time when a man has to decide if he will do something for his country ...'

'Do you realize', Jim interrupted quietly, 'that I am not an American?'

There were a few seconds of silence on the phone before an explosion of anger. 'Goddamn these bastards! I've scoured a two-inch-thick dossier and nowhere does it say anything about your not being an American!'

'Well,' Jim said, still not certain what the right move would be, 'would you be able to change my nationality so that I could do the job?'

'I'll check.'

A few days later Jim was notified that it would not be possible.

In 1991, however, he was asked to be a civilian member of the US Department of Defense Scientific Advisory Board, concerned with software in the Air Force, the only non-American on the board. At that stage the Air Force was spending approximately $30 billion a year on software and it was being predicted that the amount would double in the *following three years even though the USSR had imploded, the Berlin Wall had come down, the Cold War was over and the spectacular Strategic Air Command had been shut down.*

On another occasion the Canadian Prime Minister's limousine was idling outside the arrival gate at Toronto Airport waiting for Jim to emerge so that he could be whisked to a consultancy assignment with the PM.

'What business are you on in Canada, Mr Martin?' the official perusing his passport enquired.

'Management consultancy,' Jim replied.

'Can't be true.'

'Why not?'

'The Prime Minister's office just announced that no foreign management consultants can be used from now on, only nationals. What are you really here for?'

'That is what I am here for.'

'So who is it that has hired you to do this consulting?'

'The Prime Minister.'

Certain that he was being mocked, the official called guards, and Jim was escorted to a cell. For three hours the limousine waited outside while Jim got on with writing his latest book, not wanting to waste an opportunity for some solitude.

By the time the mess had been sorted out and he had met with the Prime Minister the story had been leaked to the press and was all over the evening news. Unable to get hold of Jim for a quote, the reporters made up their own stories.

'James Martin basks in the sunshine on his Bermudian beach house and, when the phone rings, takes off in his private jet to give advice to prime ministers at $50,000 a shot.'

The following morning the Toronto Globe and Mail *ran a large cartoon showing ranks of bewildered-looking people leaving a seminar room. The caption read 'The seminar ended. The bureaucrats retired from the room in silent confusion. For fifty thousand and expenses their lives had been changed but it would be years before they would understand how ...'*

In India in 1988 Prime Minister Rajiv Gandhi (son of the assassinated Mrs Gandhi) developed the belief that there must be possibilities for building software factories in his country and was advised to call in Jim for a consultation. Gandhi had been a computer programmer himself and had a vision of developing software companies with hordes of Indians sitting in front of screens, coding, testing, writing or merely key-punching. Jim was shocked by how overworked and harassed the Prime Minister seemed. He had an official in charge of technology who was called Sam Pitroda, a man who looked like Rasputin in a biblical robe, hair down to his waist and bare feet, but sounded like a streetwise Chicago entrepreneur. Born in poverty in India, Sam had somehow managed to build a company in Chicago that created software for telephone switching computers, selling the company for many millions of dollars before returning to India.

'Our problem is simple,' the Prime Minister told Jim. 'We need to find ways to earn enough money to feed a population that is growing at the rate of about one person every second.'

It took longer than the Prime Minister would have wanted, but India did eventually manage to become a centre for building software.

In 2000, James Martin & Company, which specialized in building highly complex systems for the securities business and finance industry, changed its name to Headstrong. By that time India was writing software of very high quality at a fraction of what it would cost in America, so Headstrong bought a large Indian software company.

The first time Jim was <u>called in to talk to the CIA was in 1983</u>, just after the Russians had shot down Korean Airlines flight 007, killing everyone on board. Jim was informed over dinner that the subject was not available for conversation.

On the executive floor where Jim was working most of the top managers looked more like pipe-smoking, tweed-jacketed Oxford dons than the spooks of fiction. They seemed to him to be deep-thinking men with diverse interests, chess-playing strategists who liked complex problems to solve, often esoteric problems divorced from reality. He soon realized, however, that operatives at both the CIA and the National Security Agency were well trained in asking questions and encouraging experts like him to 'dump' whatever knowledge they had, but they never revealed anything in exchange, which limited the amount they were ultimately able to learn.

Two television companies had approached Jim while he was at IBM, asking if he would be willing to make educational programmes for universities based on his writings. The blossoming performer in Jim loved the idea of learning how to present to the camera, but IBM had decided it was a step too far and wouldn't allow it. Now that he was free to please himself Jim approached the two companies again with suggestions of how he would like the programmes to be structured and asking for part ownership of the company that he eventually agreed to work with.

If he were able to make the programmes as he wanted, it would be a massive venture, eventually involving the creation of two hundred and forty multimedia products. In the end he went with Deltak, who offered him options to buy six per cent of the company. The tapes, some of which would later become disks, were to be leased to companies all over the world on a monthly rental and were designed to build up into a library. The enormous amount of back-up written material was mostly taken from Jim's existing books and in an attempt to cut down on his travelling time he arranged for most of the shooting to be done at the house in Bermuda.

Always looking for new ways to use the media better, Jim was the first person in the world to make an educational product on laser disk and then the first interactive educational laser disk. This led to the linking of computers to laser disks and the creation of hypermedia, for which he had software created. This in turn led him to exploring the possibilities of building artificial intelligence into documents and creating an electronic version of a book with computer pictures, sound and chunks of television included. Practising exactly what he preached, he was constantly looking for ways to change and develop his basic products.

As long as Corinthia was tiny it was relatively easy for the whole family to travel to wherever the seminars were being held. As she grew from a toddler into a small child it became harder and the strains of always being on the road began to affect Jim's marriage. Charity and Jim separated and Corinthia stayed with her mother. But when Charity began to show signs of becoming ill Jim found himself torn, worried about whether he should be taking control of Corinthia and about how he would be able to continue to do his job properly if he did.

In 1979 Jim was at Frankfurt Airport, about to catch a flight to Tehran where he was booked to do another seminar, when he received an urgent cable.

'Do not go to Tehran,' the cable told him. 'Do not get on the plane. There is a revolution going on there. You will be arrested the moment you disembark.'

Despite the fact that he prided himself on never having missed a single lecture, Jim decided to heed the advice until he found out more and did not board the flight. What he found out was that the Shah of Iran had been overthrown and the Ayatollah Khomeini was flying out from Paris to take over the reins of power.

The two men who had been responsible for hosting Jim's forthcoming seminar had been arrested. They were employees of EDS, a company owned by Ross Perot, another larger-than-life character who also happened to be a neighbour of Jim's in Tucker's Town. Perot was not a man to sit back and wait for the politicians to sort things out. He created a small private army over the following months and sent them into Tehran to rescue his people. The mission didn't go entirely to plan, as the prisoners had been moved to a different jail to the one Perot's soldiers had created a mock-up of in order to rehearse, but they still got the men out and created a headline-grabbing international incident that would eventually provide the material for Ken Follett's bestseller On Wings of Eagles.

The Iranian Revolution was having an even more dramatic effect on Lillian, who at the time was married to the head of the Iranian stock exchange. The first she knew of the trouble was when a tank appeared on the front lawn with the gun turret pointing directly at her windows.

Her four children's passports were confiscated, but she found a diplomatic route to smuggle them out to America. There were hate slogans painted across the walls of the house. She eventually managed to escape herself and met up with the children again in California. Her husband elected to stay in Tehran in order to try to rebuild his life under the new regime and Lillian found herself living and working as an editor in Los Angeles, struggling to support and educate her children as a single mother.

Tragically, Charity's illness grew worse and she died. Because both she and Jim had been only children there were no aunts or uncles or cousins to come forward and provide support. Mabel had died in 1977 and Tom just a year later. Corinthia then had no relative but Jim, and Jim had no relative but Corinthia.

CHAPTER THIRTEEN
Meeting the Guru

In 1989 I was commissioned by publishers McGraw-Hill to write a book about a company called James Martin Associates (JMA). Although I had written a fair amount about general business subjects for management and marketing magazines I knew virtually nothing about technology and had never heard of James Martin. The editor at McGraw-Hill, however, convinced me that it would be an interesting learning curve. He was right.

James Martin had created a rigorous discipline called Information Engineering for the design and construction of complex systems using computers. A man called Tony Carter wanted to create a consultancy based on Information Engineering. The two men were exact opposites. Where Jim was shy and quietly spoken, Tony was confident and ebullient. Tony was a devoted and battle-scarred rugby player while Jim consciously avoided taking any physical exercise that wasn't 'gentle and pleasant', such as walking or swimming. 'If I feel the need for exercise coming on,' he said, 'I go to sleep until the feeling goes away.'

Despite their differences the two men hit it off. The deal was done and the consultancy was launched with dramatic results. The company was set up in 1983, after Jim had published a variety of books relating to the subject. The James Martin methodology addressed the rigorous definition of data and the means of ensuring accuracy and consistency of deployment of processes and Jim had published a bestselling three-volume work called *Information Engineering*. When laid side by side a beautiful fractal picture spread across the jackets of the three books. Later he published *An Information Systems Manifesto*, which became one of the most influential books in the industry. Tony felt that he needed someone whose authority in the field would be indisputable.

The resulting company, James Martin Associates, developed and promulgated Jim's well-known concepts on large systems and provided consultancy to many major companies. The focus of that work was on the reason why so many large systems fail. Despite the input of correct data and the embedding of well-proven processes, faults in logic could nevertheless result in catastrophic failure.

By this stage Jim was practiced at playing the part of the IT guru, dressing and grooming himself to look like the powerful business people he was advising. He went to a Savile Row tailor. It was almost like he was putting on a costume in order to cover up the real him and disguise the shyness that still made him seem awkward when he was offstage in social situations. He wanted to do everything possible to give weight to the ideas he was putting before his audiences and had reasoned that if he looked like a scruffy university professor they might dismiss him as not understanding the realities of the world that they inhabited.

In order to remain the most successful operator in his business he had to continue learning all the time. The most successful guru was the fastest learner and that became easier with age and experience (just as Bertrand Russell had told him all those years before). One of the best ways to learn is to consult, since the very nature of the work means that you become privy to the problems that are besetting the market, and have to apply solutions that create realistic results. The more widely his net could be cast around the world in search of problems and solutions, the more detailed and far-reaching his knowledge was becoming.

Many of Jim's predictions throughout the 1970s and 1980s had by this stage proved to be remarkably close to the mark and they had established a reputation for him as a seer or guru (words he hated because of their spiritual, otherworldly connotations). Because he had been right so many times in the past, people felt obliged to take everything he said seriously. When a big company in the technology market missed a future trend it risked missing out on billions of dollars worth of market share and falling hopelessly behind the competition. If talking to Jim for a couple of days might help them to avoid that danger they were happy to pay whatever fee he asked. Tony Carter had realized that if, while talking to them, Jim saw that what they needed was an ongoing consultancy service to build a methodology that would actually work, then he would be able to pass them on to others with more detailed, specialist knowledge and the time to implement it. Tony built the team to fulfil that role.

Jim had already seen enough of consultancy in America to know that Tony's ambitious plans for selling information engineering services in Europe could work well. Within five years the company was doing well enough to be able to convince McGraw-Hill that they should publish a book about it, which we would eventually entitle *An Extraordinary Business*.

Familiarizing myself with the business meant that I had to spend a fair bit of time interviewing people within the company, but the figure of James Martin himself remained distant and almost mythological. People spoke in awe of the predictions he had made in his early books that had duly come true, and of the great fortune that he was amassing as a result. They talked of the inspiring seminars, the giant book sales figures and the beach house in Bermuda. They talked of an international figure who hob-nobbed with presidents and kings, commanding astronomical fees for his time.

Towards the end of the research period, when I was about to sit down and start to write, it was announced that Jim would be arriving at JMA's new offices outside London and that he would be giving a condensed version of one of his seminars. I duly turned up on the Friday afternoon when the 'modern-day prophet' was due to appear amongst us.

A string quartet was playing in the foyer and there was a palpable air of excitement. We were all there to see a show. On the wall above the musicians, curtains had been pulled back to reveal a portrait, double life size, of an evangelical figure. He was a man in his middle years with his arms open in a gesture of explanation and welcome. The arms seemed to be guiding people into a world of globalization and infinite possibilities. This was how I described my initial exposure to Jim in the resulting book.

On stage James Martin is a showman. He enjoys performing. He likes to shock his audiences with facts and projections about how life and business will be in the predictable future, and he aims to send them away fired with enthusiasm, floating on a cloud of adrenalin which will lead to action. The secret of his success is that he is able to generate excitement about subjects which most people find a bore and a necessary evil. He has been able to 'turn on' top management to computing, at the very highest levels.

He talks about microelectronics and genetic engineering. He tells of chips doubling their capacity every year and a half and of the development of chips with networks of neurons, like the neurons in the human brain. He explains how small silicon chips are being replaced by large chips and ultimately wafers, and how they will evolve into nanotechnology units. He awakens the audience to the possibilities of worldwide networks linking millions of computers, of microbiology, robots and mass-production factories operating largely without workers. He talks about optical fibres which can transmit the whole of Shakespeare in a quarter of a second and computers for artificial intelligence 10,000 times faster than those of today.

To illustrate his points, and to make them understandable to the audience, he describes the possible social consequences of these developments in terms of new employment and a widening division between 'them and us'. He makes predictions like the cost of 100-kiloton nuclear bombs falling to $100,000, and then sketches out the implications for world peace. He can move seemingly effortlessly between subjects, able to create patterns which link Star Wars defense systems with satellite television, nuclear fusion and the population explosion.

Tony Carter had hired a man who made his reputation directing pop concerts. He shipped in a structure from Holland designed for a rock star. During the show lights flashed and popped, audio visual images flickered, expanded and faded, clouds of dry ice billowed over the stage. There were six linked projectors for Jim's intricate slides. The marketing people had been slaving long nights over a new audiovisual show. They were unbelievably tense with pre-show nerves and exhausted from their night of preparations and rehearsals.

Jim raced in from Heathrow Airport. He did a run through with the slides and they wouldn't work. The six linked projectors refused to synchronize correctly. Members of the audience were already arriving. Tony Carter made enraged chewing motions. Everyone was in a total panic except Jim.

'No problem,' he said, 'I'll do it without slides.'

'You will absolutely not!' yelled Tony.

'Watch me. Cut the mechanical aids.'

The staff were utterly horrified, but the show had to go on. The rock music blared, searchlights swept through the smoke and Jim appeared on the front of the stage. He was silent, studying the audience faces.

'Making the adrenaline flow in an audience is like seducing a woman,' he says.

He gave the performance entirely from memory with no slides, watching the audience at every step. At the end the audience exploded into a standing ovation.

Jim has done seminars with a fever of 103°F, with a blinding headache, with broken ribs, once when his front teeth had been knocked out, when the airline had lost his clothes, and once when the stage collapsed. Even if he was chronically ill in the morning he would find he felt better after a day on stage. He never, ever, missed a show, or was late.

'In Hong Kong a number 9 typhoon signal went up', he says, 'and the audience still stayed.'

A decade earlier one of his predictions was that the world's top teachers would eventually make as much money as top film stars and then personally made the prediction come true.

Before Jim flew back out of England I managed to grab an hour or two with him in the office, and we hit it off.

'I'm going back to my house in Bermuda next,' he said. 'Why don't you come over and we can talk in more detail.'

That was how I came to be in Tuppenny House with Jim and Corinthia twenty years ago.

🌐

The stability of the Tucker's Town housing market returned in the years after Jim bought Tuppenny House. All the nearby houses had long histories of having been owned by Hollywood personalities like Joan Crawford and Glynis Johns, or famous business tycoons. Once the market had settled down more building work was done and it began to look as if Beverly Hills had been transplanted on to a tropical island. Many of the owners of the sprawling Tucker's Town mansions only ever came to the island for a few days' relaxation when the strains of New York, Los Angeles or Dallas proved too great. When they were there they remained on the private beaches and round swimming pools hidden behind high hedges of neatly trimmed hibiscus and oleander. The only people to be seen most of the time were the armies of maids and gardeners who kept the mansions in perfect order for their owners' fleeting visits. The paths that joined the mansions together and led to the sweeping greens of the golf club were as quiet as farm tracks in the middle of nowhere.

Tuppenny House itself, however, was a hive of activity, visitors constantly arriving and staying to talk about the future of technology and the phone permanently ringing. At the time when his marriage to Charity was ending and he was finding the separation from Corinthia hard to bear, Jim was also becoming worried that he was packing too much work and travel into his schedule and was not leaving himself enough time to read and think about the future. He knew that in order to stay in demand as a writer and a lecturer he needed to ensure he was constantly ahead of other people on the learning curve. Bertrand Russell's words about being able to learn faster as he got older still echoed in his memory, but he needed to cut himself off from the world for at least a few months every year to study and learn and think.

On the South Island of New Zealand he found himself a simple sheep farmer's cottage that provided him with the ultimate hideaway, miles from anywhere with only one unreliable phone line. The phone had a three-digit number. The cottage was surrounded by beautiful ecology-rich walks and Jim would sometimes be pushing his way through wild areas full of lupins practically as tall as him, overwhelmed by their perfume. There were thousands of sheep. Hummingbirds came to take syrup from a feeder and he found that if he sat dead still with a small red flower wedged behind the bridge of his reading glasses, they would hover in front of his face, taking pollen from the flower with their long tongues, allowing him to see every detail of their delicate feathering. It seemed to him to be the most beautiful place on earth, particularly at the time of year when the northern hemisphere was cold.

In the cottage he wrote his book An Information Systems Manifesto, *soon to be on the shelf of almost every IT executive in the world.*

CHAPTER FOURTEEN
Climate Change Cities

'Have you read *The Bottom Billion*?' Jim asked as we walked down an avenue of Washington palms that linked one of the house decks to the ruins of the nineteenth-century military latrine at the water's edge.

'I have,' I said.

We strolled on to the beach and across to the rocky promontory that stretched out into the glittering blue waters. We reached the furthermost bench on the island and sat down. We had both donned wide-brimmed hats and dark glasses to protect ourselves from the glare of the sun and must have looked like a pair of bookends to the passengers on the passing pleasure boats, many of whom waved at us cheerfully and pointlessly. Jim appeared not to notice any of them.

'The author is a friend of mine from Oxford,' he continued, 'Paul Collier, and he gives a brilliant analysis of why poverty is such a persistent problem in a handful of countries, most of them in Africa. While the rest of us will be growing richer and more technologically advanced at a dizzying speed in the twenty-first century, these people will remain stuck in the fourteenth, and may even slip further back into a terrible repeat of the Dark Ages. I don't agree with many of Paul's suggested solutions at the end of the book because I think most of them have been tried and have failed, but he explains exactly why we are failing in these countries. I also think there is a "bottom two billion" or more. I think Paul is probably drawing the line at people living on less than a dollar a day, but there are huge numbers living on less than two dollars a day as well who are on just as much of a slippery slope.'

Jim divides the world into four sections: the 'First World' consists of the wealthy industrial nations and about a billion people. The 'Second World' contains the vigorous nations like China and India and about three billion people who are striving to climb the ladder from poverty to 'First World' status. The 'Third World' consists of the developing countries who have been referred to in those terms for a long time, but who are beginning to climb out. Below them, however, he believes there is a 'Fourth World' of destitute countries unable to escape from the burden of poverty. At the current rates of growth he thinks the Third World could well contain three billion people by the middle of this century, and the Fourth World could be struggling to support as many as two billion.

In his book Collier lists the main causes of continued poverty in all these countries as being a mixture of civil wars, frequent coups and regime changes, hopeless levels of corruption, the curse of natural resources that create unsustainable booms that are inevitably followed by tragic busts, a lack of education and often geographical features like being landlocked and surrounded by unhelpful neighbours.

'So what is the future for the bottom billion?' I asked.

'Well.' It was impossible to read his expression behind the dark glasses as he stared out to sea, his tone matter-of-fact and unemotional. 'It's very bleak indeed unless rich countries cooperate to make vigorous changes. The shanty towns are growing to the size of cities, some of them containing millions of people, with no rule of law and no education for the young people. They're pretty much run by the local mafias.

'The problem with all the new wealth that we will be creating in the future is that it will be unevenly distributed.

Most of it will be based largely on products of the intellect, so the vast majority of the rewards will go to countries that are already richer and better educated, while the poorer countries will skid into deeper poverty unless a well-planned effort is made to prevent this.

'The gap between rich and poor will become infinitely worse when the age of The Singularity arrives because the underdeveloped world is not even able to harness today's technology effectively, so they can hardly be expected to benefit from the developments that are on the way. As the benefits are multiplying at an exponential rate in the developed world, the undeveloped world is bound to keep on sliding backwards – and then we will have the added disasters brought about by climate change, which the developed world will be able to survive due to technological advances.'

'But won't climate change affect the whole globe?'

'Of course. The results will be terrible, especially if we don't do anything to change our behaviour quickly. But picture the very real world shown in the movie *Slumdog Millionaire*, and then imagine what it will be like when that area descends into famine. In the developed world we can adapt to changes rapidly. We'll be able to build what I like to call "climate-change cities". As temperatures rise, some parts of the globe will become more pleasant and fertile and habitable than they have been in the past, just as others will become deserts or will disappear beneath rising sea levels.

'As it becomes pleasanter to live in places like the north of Finland, Russia or Canada, or the south of Patagonia, we will start to move in those directions, using all our money and skills to build the most wonderful new climate-change cities, which will be designed to take advantage of renewable power sources like wind, solar and wave power, and safe forms of nuclear power. We will be able to design the buildings to catch and use fresh rain water effectively and to be efficient in their use of resources. They could be the most beautiful places to live, but the shanty towns in the Third and Fourth Worlds will have become unspeakably worse as the desert encroaches on farmland and increasing numbers of freak weather conditions like hurricanes and floods spread destruction and disease. Many parts of the world will run out of water and much of Africa will become a desert.

'James Lovelock, the legendary expert on this, believes that by the end of the century no more than five hundred million people will be able to survive on the planet. Now, even if he is being overly pessimistic and the planet could support two billion of us, that is still less than a third of the population we have today.'

As the boats kept on passing my arm was growing tired from waving back politely to every smiling tourist and I stopped, trying to concentrate on the picture that he was describing of a world divided between utopias for the rich and dystopias for the wretched masses in the bottom few billion. I gazed for a while at the longtails as they swooped and soared above us.

'Is it possible to build whole cities that quickly?' I asked eventually.

'When the will is there it is perfectly possible. Dubai was basically built in eight years. Many of the fundamental ideas behind it are flawed, like its appalling reliance on the motor car, which makes most of the city very unpleasant to live in because it has roads like racetracks that you can't walk across. And it's in completely the wrong place for a climate-change city, but it was still built very fast to serve a purpose. Imagine a city full of architecture as imaginative as the best buildings in Dubai, designed to function without the motor car, that is full of pleasant, tranquil parklands and surrounded by fertile farmlands capable of supplying most of the food needed by the city's population.'

As I pictured the sort of place he was describing I felt myself being infected with his enthusiasm at the prospect.

The 21st Century School has an institute studying cities of the future, just as it has one studying the car of the future.

'Another of the subjects we have been studying at Oxford', Jim went on, 'is mass migration. It is already a huge problem for governments in the First World. The Americans are building a wall between them and Mexico that is going to be more impenetrable than the Iron Curtain ever was. Europe will have to guard its borders against people attempting to escape from poverty across the sea from north Africa as well as those coming in from the less-developed countries in the East. It is a terrible source of potential future conflict and we really need to be thinking about it seriously, planning how we are going to deal with the problems humanely.'

One of Jim's most frequently repeated mantras is that education has to be one of the cornerstones of any plan to save our civilization from chaos. Aware of just how far it has brought him from the life that his parents led, he believes fervently that improving education globally should be our primary goal; that it is the rain and sunshine needed by the soil of the future, and that all other good things will eventually spring from it.

One of the possible scenarios that he envisages for Africa is to create cities of the future, to which the brightest children in the shanty towns could be sent.

'They would need to be built somewhere safe,' he says. 'and laid out with a forty-year strategy, starting with a low budget but with concrete plans for where further funding would come from as they develop. The shanty towns would then be searched for exceptionally bright children. The intent in the beginning would be to select them before they were even two years old. It is often not difficult to spot precocious, exceptionally bright children.

'It is rare in the shanty towns for such children to have both parents. Often they have only a mother. But if there are parents, they would be offered the chance to move from their destitute shanty town to the new city with their child. The parents would be taught to read and given jobs building the infrastructure of the city while the child was being educated. It would become a clean, sanitary, environmentally correct city without cars, but with excellent urban transportation, perhaps like Curitiba in Brazil.

'There could be large-field solar energy sites and the ability to generate fuel for fuel cells and there would be high-bandwidth internet capability going to every building. Each child would be given an iPod, and to help them learn English (whether it is their first or second language) they would be able to replay favourite clips from films and music in English. They would be able to receive good healthcare. Hopefully, by the time these children are forty, when The Singularity will have occurred, they will have been educated in relevant material and will become entrepreneurs who will be able to go back to the shanty towns to help them develop.

'After The Singularity, people will be employed very differently from today, and education needs to take that into account.'

Beyond their basic education, Jim envisages that these young people would be taught about nanotechnology, biotechnology, future computing and networks, and stem-cell-based regenerative medicine. It would be an education of intense creativity, teaching them that unethical behaviour is not an option.

'There would be an emphasis on creating lives that have value and meaning.'

When researching his book on *The Meaning of the 21st Century*, Jim interviewed Michael Porter at the Harvard Business School who lamented the fact that the First World wasn't doing more to help the poor.

'We have the knowledge to do things better,' Porter told him. 'We know how to deal with health, deal with hunger, deal with bad water. There's been no time in history when the opportunity to deal with the poor and end poverty has been greater. Yet it isn't happening.'

Despite all his worldly success, Jim still found it hard to make the sort of small talk that helps men to meet women easily. Charity's death and the end of his marriage had left a painful hole in his life, which he mostly managed to fill with his work and with Corinthia.

Small talk was always easier for him when he was with people who shared his passions for technology and the future and in 1980 Jim met Dr Carma McClure, a diminutive and dynamic software expert, at a business dinner thrown by Deltak, the producers of Jim's videos, for whom she was a scriptwriter. She had a PhD in complexity theory, but Jim noticed she had difficulty making her microwave oven work. 'The time display on her VCR always read "12.00".'

Jim also met Lillian, who had been deputed to look after him by a seminar organizer on a trip to Los Angeles. Lillian, having successfully escaped from Tehran with her children by then, was supporting herself and her family in any way she could, partly by writing and editing in the software industry.

Jim struck up relationships with both women and co-wrote several books with Carma, inviting her to be a guest lecturer on his world seminars, which meant they were often travelling together in the same way he had once done with Charity. They also found that they shared similar tastes for both culture and adventure, sometimes with potentially dangerous results.

The weekend before an African seminar they took a break at a private game reserve in the north of South Africa. Despite the fact that it was pouring with rain there for the first time in years, they arranged one evening to go out to look for some big game in a Land Rover with two other couples, one from England the other an elderly Israeli husband and wife. They had a driver and a local spotter with an extraordinary knowledge of animals. He sat in the back with a narrow spotlight and would snap his fingers to attract the passengers' attention whenever he saw something that he believed would interest them.

It was almost completely dark, and still pouring with rain, when they reached a low bridge over the Sand River, which would take them back to the camp. The spotter snapped his fingers to attract their attention to a group of hippos who were wallowing in the water beside the bridge. As they watched the animals, Jim noticed out of the corner of his eye that the spotter was becoming agitated and seemed to be straining his eyes, trying to see up the river. As he grew more alarmed he started to shout at the driver and the tourists realized that he was saying the hippos should not have been by the bridge. The fact that they were there suggested that somewhere further upstream the river had burst loose, flooded their usual pond and washed the giant animals downstream. The shouts of both men and the urgent revving of the engine were suddenly drowned out as a mighty wave came down over the bridge, swirling angrily round their tyres.

Panicking, the driver tried to reverse, but the wheels were spinning helplessly in the mud and the engine stalled. Before he could re-start it the water level was over the exhaust pipe and it was too late.

'Everybody out!' he shouted, jumping into the water.

'Get out! Get out now! Get to the high ground!'

To reach safety they were going to have to wade through what had now become a raging torrent.

'I'm not getting out,' the Israeli woman told Jim. 'I'll be safer here.'

'That is the worst thing you could do,' Jim shouted, dragging her from her seat.

The woman became entangled in a cable running to the spotter's searchlight and by the time Jim had freed her the water was up to his chest and he could hear the others screaming. Grabbing the woman with one hand and her husband with the other he summoned all his strength to pull them through the water.

'I'm going!' Carma screamed somewhere in the darkness and part of him wanted to drop the other two and go after her, but his survival instincts had taken over and he continued dragging the elderly couple through the torrent while behind them the Land Rover was turned over by the force of the current, the beams of its headlights cutting through the black sky, lighting up the intense rain for a few seconds before being swallowed up and swept away.

The water had reached Jim's neck and was trying to pull him back from the bank, which seemed to be getting further and further away. The old woman was at least a foot shorter than him and her head kept disappearing beneath the surface. It was taking all his strength to keep hauling her back up. They felt submerged bushes around their legs and clung to them as they tried to pull themselves forward and finally dragged themselves out on to dry land.

Jim laid the couple on the ground. The woman coughed up water, gasping for breath, but her husband was still and silent, felled at some stage of the struggle by a fatal heart attack. The other members of the group were shouting to one another in the dark, gradually reassembling, and Jim felt a wave of relief when he heard Carma's voice. He and the driver tried in vain to pump life back into the old man's body before rigor mortis started to set in and they knew they had lost the battle.

Huddled in the darkness the survivors shivered and tried to work out what to do next. They had no lights, not even matches, no radio, no cell phones and no guns and they *could hear the roaring of lions in the distance. All Jim had in his pocket was a Swiss Army knife, which the spotter asked to borrow, disappearing into the blackness, leaving them in the rain with no idea if they would ever see him again. When he reappeared he was carrying some eight-foot spears that he had cut from the undergrowth.*

A few hours later another Land Rover, sent out from the camp to search for them, appeared on the horizon. There wasn't room for all of them so the first driver volunteered to stay with the dead man until they could send more help and the spotter vanished into the jungle, afraid now that he would be blamed for the catastrophe.

'The river has risen twelve feet,' the second driver shouted as he helped the rest of them into the back. 'It's moving like a tidal wave, we have to hurry and get ahead of it.'

Once they were all safely on board, lying on the floor, he sped off over land in a last attempt to race the water so they could cross the river back to the camp. The branches of bushes and trees tore the windshield off and whipped at their faces and the wind had become as cold as ice. For some reason Carma had brought a handful of shower caps with her from the camp in case of emergencies and now, as they ploughed on through the jungle, she kept pulling them on to her head, one after another, as fast as the undergrowth tore them off.

After more than an hour they attempted to cross the river again, but the tidal wave was too close on their tails and the water levels were rising too fast. They had to reverse back out and take off again until they reached a ford, which still seemed to be shallow enough for them to cross in safety. In the distance they could hear the angry roar of the wave as it raced to catch them up and cut off this final escape route.

'This is the last chance we have,' the driver shouted as he drove in and the water came up to the vehicle's axles. Careful not to stall the engine he ploughed steadily across

as the water rose behind them. The wheels eventually got a grip of the bank on the other side and suddenly they were being pulled up and out to safety.

They eventually drove into the camp at three in the morning. The staff had prepared the best meal possible and had filled their bathtubs with hot water. Jim climbed into his with a glass of cognac in his hand, which at that moment seemed like the best he had ever tasted. Fifteen minutes later he was still shivering, despite the heat of the water.

The next day he and Carma flew out and were both back on stage as though nothing had happened. The show had to go on, as always.

CHAPTER FIFTEEN
Nuclear Sanity

'Nuclear power is a big question that we really have to think about more sensibly,' Jim said as we sat one evening on the western side of the island with a bottle of wine on the stone table in front of us and the sky turning orange as the sun sank behind the mainland.

It's another of the subjects that he is passionate about. He has written a book, with the working title *Insanity*, that paints a chilling picture of how close the human race has been to wiping itself out with nuclear weapons and suggests that future nuclear crises will be fundamentally different from those of the past.

'A few years ago we were having a party here,' he said. 'The moon was full but there was suddenly a much brighter light out there over the sea. It looked like it was miles away. It hovered in the sky long enough for all of us to see it, then a second one joined it and hovered for a moment before they streaked off into the southerly sky, gaining speed as they went and leaving a strange, grey haze hanging over the sea, which lasted about ten minutes.

'It was a perfect flying saucer story,' he grinned. 'I didn't dare tell anybody, because they'd say "we've heard strange stories about Gunpowder Island".

'The next day the Bermuda papers were full of stories about UFOs. One newspaper reported Bermudians describing how they had been captured by aliens. Three days later, a new news story was published. The USS *West Virginia*, an

Ohio class submarine, was testing two D5 missiles. The first stage of each missile is fired under the sea. Because rough waves on the surface may deflect their course slightly, they are designed to hover above the water while detailed adjustments are made to the trajectory, and then the second stage of the missile is fired. The missile moves slowly at first and then accelerates as its solid-state rocket blasts it into the sky. They are incredibly accurate, able to hit targets that are thousands of miles away.

'Those two missiles we saw had sixteen re-entry vehicles in total, each with separate targets and each designed to carry an atomic warhead with almost forty times the explosive power of the bomb that destroyed Hiroshima. That submarine was carrying twenty-four of those missiles, so in theory it could vaporize one hundred and ninety-two cities.'

In his new book Jim describes the technologies and procedures necessary for the command and control of nuclear crises, and the alarming prospect that it is now possible to automate a massive nuclear strike involving thousands of simultaneous launches. New technology, he explains, is bringing about the biggest changes ever seen in the military, creating new dangers as nuclear weapons and delivery mechanisms drop in cost and take on new forms. He describes the era ahead as the 'Age of Amorphousness', amorphous implying shapeless, unpredictable, with no clear structure, with unexpected networks, coming from anywhere, no rules.

'Expect the unexpected,' he says. 'In Cole Porter's words, "Anything Goes".

'Fighting in the future may not be between countries, it may be between religions, or ideologies, non-state actors, terrorist organizations, global mafias, or fanatic groups that want to change the world. The only way to be safe in the Age of Amorphousness is to have a global treaty for eliminating nuclear weapons. Whether this happens in five years or fifty years, it is an essential part of the twenty-first century.

'We have reached a time in which there will either be no all-out war between high-tech nations or there will be no civilization. Weapons of mass destruction can now be produced in such large quantities at such low costs that a nuclear or biological war would bring our civilization down like a pack of cards. We are dependent on infrastructures of immense complexity, all of which would collapse.

'If a war between high-tech nations was to start it would probably happen like a flash fire. Cybernetic attacks could put numerous essential computers out of action. The military would want to fire every nuclear weapon they have and, possibly, massive quantities of biological weapons too. The devastation would be unlike anything we can even imagine.

'The challenge is to achieve enough mutual understanding and respect amongst different civilizations that war and terrorism become less likely. In the past, civilizations have held beliefs so passionately that they have been willing to go to war for them. We now have a growing foundation layer of global understanding, but it is still immature.

'If the world is not to fall into increasingly horrifying conflicts it has to keep increasing multicultural tolerance and respect.

'The grand irony of our time is that unspeakably evil systems were built by good people practising their disciplines. The professionals working on software methodologies for the Department of Defense have their heads full of the detailed problems and challenges of their work. They don't think about the bigger picture. In the past they didn't think about how civilization might have ended if we hadn't been lucky.

'Utterly brilliant people can often build houses of cards. We saw it with the complex products created in the banking system, which all collapsed so fast. The confrontation of tens of thousands of nuclear weapons was another house of cards. It was just luck that nothing triggered their use.

'On Sundays some members of the Department of Defense Scientific Advisory Board used to go to church during the time I was with them. There would be all these two-star generals kneeling down and praying, and one told me afterwards that he had prayed for forgiveness for not tipping a taxi driver the previous week. That same Sunday the sermon was all about avoiding the pomp and vanity of the world, not about preventing the end of civilization.'

Jim is not naïve enough to think for a moment that we have seen the end of wars, but only that they will be limited to countries who are not yet part of the 'high-tech club', as he puts it.

'But we mustn't underestimate the human capacity for pure evil,' he explained. 'The massive intercontinental ballistic missiles may remain very expensive, but simple versions of weapons of mass destruction will become even cheaper and easier to make because of advances in technology. Bright kids will have plans they've found in some cranny of the internet showing how to make a simple atomic bomb. It will be as easy to make as a lawnmower if you follow the plans very carefully and if you have the enriched uranium. We must make sure they don't get the enriched uranium. A genius kid in a garage will be able to concoct genetically modified pathogens. Two young laboratory workers in Australia created a genetically modified mouse pox, which killed every mouse it touched. We could probably do that with human smallpox. There are multiple ways in which we could destroy our civilization.'

Despite these fears, all of them based on meticulous historical research, Jim still believes that nuclear power is our best chance of keeping the lights of civilization on while slowing down the potential progress of catastrophic climate change.

'We have got to get more electricity but less carbon out of the atmosphere,' he insisted as he re-filled our wine glasses. 'So we're totally dependent on having enough non-carbon energy. No other source of non-carbon energy can be big enough or created fast enough. We are now seeing a major resurgence of nuclear power, but it has to be rigorously separated from the ability to produce nuclear weapons.

'We have got to find a new maturity and stop all these knee-jerk reactions to the words "nuclear power". Nuclear weapons are incredibly dangerous, nuclear power isn't. In the US alone forty-four thousand people a year die because of coal power stations – many from respiratory diseases. No one is killed by nuclear power. We have got to grasp that fact and think clearly if we want to move forward.

'To make the grade today a nuclear power station has to meet certain criteria. No matter what mistakes the operators might make the power stations are safe and the spent fuel can be disposed of so that it leaves no radioactive problems for future generations.'

Jim is particularly enthusiastic about a new type of system for generating electricity and hydrogen, known as 'pebble-bed reactors', in which the uranium fuel is entirely enclosed in a spherical casing, like a tiny ball bearing. These spheres are ultra-strong and have a four-layer shell that can withstand very high pressures and temperatures. The ball cannot be crushed, corroded or melted. There are many of them inside a sphere the size of a billiard ball, which is called the pebble. There is no possibility of uranium dust spreading.

I had heard him enthusing about them at a seminar in Oxford, during which he passed around a plastic bag with both billiard balls and similar-looking pebbles. In the gunpowder vaults on Gunpowder Island there is a snooker table, and some games have these pebbles nestling amongst the normal snooker balls. It creates an interesting image of the great guru delightedly playing with uranium balls in his secret underground island hideaway. It is easy to get swept up in the eccentric magic of Jim's world.

'Watch the water,' Jim said, suddenly changing the subject and pointing down to the sea beneath where we were sitting. It had grown dark while we were talking, the sun having finally set nearly an hour earlier, and the sky was lit only with stars.

As we studied the black waters of the bay below hundreds of white and green points of light were suddenly swirling in circles.

'They're fire worms', Jim said, 'going through a mating ritual. It only happens here in Bermuda. Three days after the full moon, once it's dark, the females swim to the surface and exude a luminous excretion. The smaller males rush to the display, spiral around the females and mate, emitting the green light.'

The tiny creatures stayed brilliantly lit for a few seconds before disappearing to the bottom and being replaced by more. The whole show lasted for about ten minutes and then they vanished, leaving us sitting in the starlight, thinking.

In 1990 Jim and Carma decided to get married in a balloon, flying at ten thousand feet over the Alps.

They stayed at Schloss Fuschl, a fairytale chateau overlooking one of Austria's grandest lakes, once used as the summer residence of the Archbishops of Salzburg.

The priest and best man went up in the balloon basket with the happy couple, along with the navigator and pilot, and a man who filmed the whole event. Carma wore a lavish, billowing white wedding dress with a long, flowing veil and had to be lifted into the basket by two men. Her veil had to be removed before they set off for fear that it would be sucked up into the flame when the hot air burner roared into action.

It was a beautiful day for ballooning, with a brilliant light and a strong wind. They travelled for forty miles, over mountains covered in deep snow, waiting until the sun was low over the mountains before the ceremony commenced and the balloon descended slowly through a dusky sunset. As the prayers were said it seemed to Jim that they were much closer to God than they ever would have been in a church.

He woke early next morning and amused himself by repeatedly playing back the video that had been shot while he waited for Carma to wake up. Much of the footage was beautiful but as he jotted down an edit list it became clear that it wouldn't edit. There were critical moments missing or pieces that wouldn't match.

'Sweetheart,' he announced to his new bride when she finally stirred, 'we've got to do it again!'

'You've got to be kidding.'

The balloon pilot and navigator were happy to fly again. The priest thought it was wicked. The best man loved the idea. It was another beautiful day, but this time the balloon headed in an entirely different direction, since no one can control the wind. When they were high enough, they filmed Carma's veil, after making sure that the hot air burner was not switched on. The trip lacked the deadly seriousness of the previous day as the couple recited their wedding vows, less tensely this time, and the best man sang songs from The Sound of Music.

Jim and Carma decided to do a seminar in Brazil, timed so that they could go to the carnival in Rio – a time when Brazilians on both sides of the country's deep social and economic divide cast aside their worries for almost a week in a frenzy of samba dancing.

The Black and White Ball was one of the most elegant events of the carnival, taking place in a hotel on the Copacabana at the heart of the greatest party on earth. Outside the hotel the streets vibrated with hundreds of wild samba schools as they weaved their joyful way around the city. The ballroom was packed with partygoers dressed in extravagant and imaginative black and white costumes, dancing through the night with no letup in the samba music or the writhing excitement of the dancers. Carma weighed only ninety pounds, so Jim could easily pick her up and swing her around him as the dancing grew ever wilder.

Jim seemed like a giant in the crowd, his towering frame topped by a tall black and white hat, like an illustration from the famous Cat in the Hat *book, as he sambaed eccentrically in a tuxedo and white cummerbund. As the crowd became more frenzied he hoisted Carma up on to his shoulders and they sambaed together, Jim holding Carma's feet as she spread her arms out wide, embracing the joy of life to the full. Back at the table to catch their breath, she looked at him with piercing eyes.*

'If you generate code from the design screen, why should it be COBOL?' she said. 'Wouldn't it be better to generate machine language?'

Jim thought about that as he felt the table pulsate with the neverending samba beat.

'Maybe C++,' he said eventually.

CHAPTER SIXTEEN
Global Warming

We were sitting under a pergola loaded down with creepers beside the ancient barracks at the far end of the island, sheltering from the sun. I was transfixed by a large green and purple lizard frozen on the twisted trunk that wound round the balustrade beside me. I could completely sympathize with its reluctance to indulge in any activity beyond blinking: I had only been on the island a week and the peace and isolation had left me almost unable to move, happy just to bask in the warmth, the sea breeze, the scents of the pittosporum and Jim's gentle company. He had been talking solidly for almost the entire week but still the ideas kept bubbling out.

From the depths of the other rickety wooden chair he was patiently explaining why global warming was more of a problem than most people so far realized. A scarlet cardinal flew on to a nearby branch and watched us for a moment. The lizard stopped even blinking.

'Imagine you are taking a shower,' Jim was saying, 'and when you turn the water on it is too cold, so you twist the knob that will warm it up. You won't feel the increase in heat immediately. There will be a delay of perhaps twenty seconds before it starts to come through and then you have time to adjust the temperature again to get it just right.

'With global warming humanity may take action to reduce greenhouse gases but again you don't feel the change immediately. This time the delay may be twenty years. It feels to the public like nothing is happening as a result of their efforts. It also means that all the politicians who are in power when a particular decision is made are probably retired by the time there is any tangible result, so there is little personal motivation for them to instigate such changes because they will enjoy none of the benefits or praise. We just have to hope that they have the wisdom to realize that the decisions they take today could make the difference between the world being a wonderful place for their grandchildren and great grandchildren, or large parts of the globe becoming uninhabitable. The only way we can know we have taken the right action is by trusting the calculations of scientists who study the subject using extremely elaborate computer models. That is why climate change is such a central part of what we are doing at Oxford.'

One of the greatest enemies of humankind throughout history has been infectious disease. The modern media is frequently overtaken with scare stories about new pandemics, predicting that they are going to decimate the global population. Their fears are not without foundation, since it is well known that twice as many people died from the flu outbreak of 1918 than had died in the First World War. In Jim's 21st Century School Angela McLean is Director of the Institute of Emerging Infections. Her staff created what are probably the world's best models of future pandemics. Angela was made a Fellow of All Souls, where Jim had met Bertrand Russell half a century before, and she was also made a Fellow of the Royal Society.

In recent times we have seen the arrival of HIV/Aids, SARS, bird flu, malaria and swine flu, all of which have struck hardest at the poorest regions of the world, where the people are least able to take precautions and can least afford to buy the necessary drugs. Changes in climate are likely to create more surprise infections in the future and the poor are going to be even more vulnerable than before.

'The worst scenario', Jim says, 'is a pandemic caused by an artificially modified pathogen that takes nature by surprise. I think it is inevitable that we will suffer from a lethal flu epidemic eventually, so we just need to be prepared to fight it. These diseases could develop naturally or could also be introduced by acts of terrorism. Nature has evolved protective mechanisms over billions of years but genetically modified pathogens would be a serious problem. In the past Russian researchers have modified smallpox, bubonic plague and other terrible diseases, keeping them in storage as potential weapons. It is now perfectly possible for a brilliant misfit in a small laboratory to do the same and create the most lethal disease agents.

'A hundred million people died directly or indirectly as a result of armed conflict in the twentieth century, but three hundred million died of smallpox. It is an awful death. The body becomes a mass of festering blisters, almost unbearably painful and so dense that the skin separates from its under layers.

'The spread of swine flu was declared a pandemic and there will inevitably be others, capable of infecting much of the world's population. Humanity could be protected from this if it had a large enough quantity of vaccines, but vaccines cannot be manufactured until the specific mutation of the disease is known. Today a vaccine would not be available until three or four months after the pandemic started, and it is likely that the quantity would be only a small fraction of what is needed. Unless far better preparations are made, the First World would not have enough vaccine for its own people, so it would be very unlikely to give any to the Third or Fourth Worlds.

'A killer pandemic is likely to take hold and then rage out of control in some of the most overpopulated cities that have bad healthcare and unsanitary conditions, like a forest fire taking advantage of dry areas of dense pine trees. Governments would then have to decide whether to quarantine cities to lessen the rate of the spread. Other countries would also inevitably close their borders and the global economy would come to a halt, creating economic damage that would compound the damage from the disease itself. If we don't make more of an effort to help the poor countries to prepare for these possible pandemics they might wipe out as many as a billion people in a frighteningly short time span.'

Jim and Carma's marriage was a meeting of like minds and good friends, but it soon became clear that they actually wanted very different lifestyles. Carma thrived on big city life and didn't share Jim's love of isolated houses and walking in the wildernesses of the world. Wanting to maintain their friendship and mutual respect they decided to end the marriage and go their separate ways after six years. It was a peaceful parting.

However much he travelled and however much time he spent in different locations, Bermuda remained Jim's base, and the more serene and manicured Tucker's Town became the more he found himself craving for a bit of wilderness on his own doorstep and somewhere to walk where there just might be some different views and surprises. He decided to go house hunting again. Bermuda still suited him geographically and felt like home, but the main island was virtually all built over and it seemed impossible to find a property that he could put his stamp on and create something that was more imaginative and exciting.

'Would you be interested in buying an island?' the real estate agent asked.

'Sure, if you have one,' Jim replied, doubting if there was anything left in Bermuda that would give him the sort of project that he was looking for even as he climbed into the boat with her.

The island the real estate agent was heading for was Gunpowder Island. It stood on the north side of a narrow channel called Two-Rock Passage, which ships bound for Hamilton would pass carefully through. The moment Jim saw it from the boat he felt the adrenaline beginning to pump through his veins. Nature had swamped the rocks that they were circling so thoroughly that it was hard to imagine how they were even going to be able to view it without a team of men walking in front of them wielding machetes.

The history of the island went back nearly four hundred years, to 1611, when the first stock exchange opened in Amsterdam, followed soon afterwards by London. Dealmakers looked for anything that could be bought and sold in the new markets and they started to sell land in the newly discovered Bermuda, with exaggerated stories about how it would rise in value. In 1613 a man called Sir Anthony Agar, with no intention of ever going near the place himself, bought one of the islands and egocentrically named it Agar's Island. This was the island Jim was now circling and to which he would quickly become attached, buying it with no idea of what he was going to find once the clearing work started in earnest.

In 1998 Jim published his hundredth book, Cybercorp. *It described in detail what a corporation should be like if it was fully designed for the age of cyberspace. Agile, virtual, global cybernetic corporations, he argued, were the wave of the future. Rather than trying to 'reengineer' old, arthritic companies, he urged business leaders to learn how to transform their companies into 'cybercorps'.*

The book touched a raw nerve in China. Tsinghua University, which is like the MIT of Beijing, translated the book into Mandarin so fast that the Chinese version came out before the American version. China was at a moment of massive transition. Its corporations were old, vast, rigid and communist – about as far away as possible from the principles and mechanisms Jim was advocating in Cybercorp. *The book had high sales in China and Jim was asked to be a "change agent", which involved being taken on a tour of the country's biggest state corporations in order to advise their leaders on how to adapt to the new world of the internet and business re-engineering.*

In Shanghai the authorities allocated Jim an old bullet-proof commissar-wagon, like a Russian version of a 1950 Lincoln Continental.

'It flew two red flags and never stopped honking,' he remembers, 'especially in no-horn zones. The driver was straight out of a Hitchcock movie. Perhaps he was a driver for the Triads. He had a crew cut and an old and brutal three-inch scar on the back of his head, but he never stopped smiling.'

China was being re-invented to be a devastating force in the world and Jim felt like he was at the centre of an intellectual tornado everywhere he went. The protocols of communism were being ripped to shreds by a brilliantly creative internet generation.

'The message was clear,' he says. 'China must skip two generations of management just as it skipped two generations of technology. Everything must be "cybercorp". But you couldn't get from where they were to where they needed to be by adjusting the procedures of a communist world. The only way ahead was to scrap the old corporations and start again – replace them with new, agile, small enterprises with young people who could turn on a dime. Set new goals and reinvent everything. Let the stars of corporate reinvention become rich.'

During the five-week tour Jim got to know many Chinese who had been victims of the Cultural Revolution. This was perhaps the first time that Chinese executives and professionals had been prepared to describe what happened to them during that time. Once they started, they would talk for hours, and the stories they told were like nightmares, making Jim shudder. They talked of how their libraries and possessions were destroyed and how they were humiliated and punished, made to strip naked and crawl through the streets on all fours like dogs, for months on end, with notices round their necks advertising that they were 'bourgeois pigs who had exploited other classes'. Many did not survive the ordeal. The Red Guards were ordered to criticize and repudiate the 'reactionary bourgeois academic authorities' and attack 'the ideology of the bourgeoisie and all other exploiting classes'.

Many temples, churches, mosques, monasteries and shrines were destroyed. Almost all universities and theatres were closed and most libraries were burnt. Over long, spicy meals, around tables with rotating glass centres, articulate Chinese described to Jim how they'd had no contact with their families for eight years, how they had been sent a thousand miles from the city and made to look after pigs or grow lettuces.

It was declared illegal to own antiques and vast junk yards grew up where priceless historical artefacts that had been confiscated were dumped in preparation for destruction. Jim asked if he could be taken round some of these junk yards and soon realized there were treasure troves of sculptures and statues hidden amongst every kind of rubbish. He could imagine how well many of these objects would fit in with the dramatic scenery of Gunpowder Island, becoming integral parts of his and Duncan's evolving plans. He collected as many as the authorities would allow, filling a container that would be shipped to Bermuda via New York.

Some of the statues that came to nestle in the island jungle are anything up to four hundred years old and look as if they have always been in the peaceful, secluded positions they now occupy. A pair of mighty, weather-beaten rams guard one set of steps to the house, a pair of lions, with moveable balls intricately carved inside their grinning mouths, stand at the entrance to the main beach, and a marble dragon curls and snarls with flared eyes and nostrils in a partially hidden water garden. There are peaceful Buddhas and angry griffins and gargoyles in every corner. Like the people Jim got to talk to, they are the lucky ones, spared from destruction during the revolution, their dignity now restored to them in their new settings.

To relax after China, Jim went on to Myanmar (formerly known as Burma), his main means of transportation a rickety bicycle-taxi with a driver who belched as he pedalled.

Although the old Burma was a world of poverty, the spirituality of the country captured his imagination. There was no internet, no Western movies and only one channel of government television, broadcasting programmes like Songs to Uphold National Spirit. *The serene countryside was full of flowers and dotted with stupas and temples, which increased the deep sense of peace and other-worldliness. Giant golden pagodas glowed red at sunset and the saffron-robed monks seemed to know something profound.*

'The ordinary people there believe their lives exist in multiple planes', Jim explained, 'and that earthly attainment is a waste of energy. Until 1995, foreigners were kept out of Burma. It was decaying, very poor, but the people were apparently happy in their spirituality. Trees grew from the windows of old colonial-style buildings and it all seemed fragile and vulnerable. I went a hundred miles into the countryside, very aware that if anything went wrong nobody would ever find me.'

In 1999, Jim met up again with Lillian. She had moved to New York to be near to her children, who were grown up by then. They started to see each other again as friends and the relationship slowly rekindled. They married in 2004 in South Africa in another very private ceremony: just the two of them and a Unitarian priest.

'It felt like we were eloping,' Jim chuckles when he remembers the day. 'We decided not to tell anyone else until afterwards.'

CHAPTER SEVENTEEN
The Bigger Picture

'The biggest difficulty for The 21st Century School', Jim said as we wrestled with the espresso machine, which seemed to have run out of water, 'is deciding which of the issues we should concentrate on because there are so many of them. The basic idea was to create an interdisciplinary school, focused on the future, with the highest academic standards, and doing deep research. It has to look at all the big problems of the twenty-first century and build an integrated view of them. Nobody in the world was doing that yet.'

Lillian and Sue were talking on the other side of the room and seemed to be ignoring us on purpose, determined that we should be made to master at least one practical task on our own, to serve our required 'daily hour' in the real world. With a lot of hissing and spitting the machine went to work and eventually the right sort of aromas began to fill the kitchen. We felt ridiculously pleased with ourselves as we waited for it to brew.

'An International Advisory Board reviews all the institutes regularly and the university examines four basic criteria,' Jim went on as we stood watching it, waiting for the lights to tell us it was ready. 'The first is the scale of the issue to be studied, which means assessing the risk factors and the opportunities on offer. With climate change and stem-cell research, for instance, it is easy to see both the risks of not doing anything and the opportunities that are possible if we get it right. Then it assesses the excellence of the people who are doing the work. They need to be the best in the world on that particular issue. It looks at the impact their work is going to have because we want to be as certain as we can be that it is going to change the world over the next ten years. And finally it examines what value can be added to their work by integrating it into an interdisciplinary school. What value can the school bring to them and what value can they bring to other people connected to the school?

'Oxford isn't necessarily the best place for every discipline. They are not, for instance, the world leaders in nuclear nonproliferation, which is why I have also forged links with the Monterey Institute, what is now the James Martin Center for Nonproliferation Studies in California. When I was starting my book on the future of nuclear weapons I scoured the world for experts on the subject and the people at Monterey seemed to be the best in the world, teaching students to become future ambassadors. What they were doing fitted in with everything we were doing in Oxford.

'So much great work has been done at Oxford over the centuries. Antibiotics were pretty much invented there, and the university was also in the forefront with the atomic bomb, radar and microwaves. If they had taken out patents on all of them they would be the wealthiest university in the world. But then everyone makes mistakes. IBM turned down the Xerox machine because they thought carbon paper did the job just fine and that no one would want to spend that much money making copies of documents. They turned down the Polaroid camera too. It's like the record companies who turned down The Beatles and the publishers who turned down *Harry Potter*. It isn't always easy to spot the big money makers at the early stages.'

The coffee was ready and we filled two cups before making our way over to the table.

'It's not always easy to spot which inventions are going to make the most dramatic changes to the way humankind lives either,' Jim continued. 'The invention of hay, for instance, made it possible for cities like London to come into existence. The Romans didn't use it because in Mediterranean climates the grass grew so well in the winter that there was no need to cut it and store it. It only came into use in the Dark Ages and it enabled the populations of northern Europe to make widespread use of horses and oxen and eventually permitted cities such as London to grow and become great centres of activity. It requires vision to spot these opportunities, and strong leadership to guide their development.'

One of the 'extraordinary things' that has happened on Jim's island is the birth of the World Education Corps. Tom Benson was the President of the Green Mountain College in Vermont.

'Tom has a divinity degree', Jim said, 'and a genius for inspiring young people, holding court in the Harvard Club in New York, telling people how to think about the twenty-first century and radiating enthusiasm.'

Together he and Jim founded the Corps, which recognized the vital importance of the T-Generation. Its goal was to pick brilliant kids from different countries around the world, give them appropriate training and send them to other countries where they could help in places like schools, non-government organizations and companies. They would be from a variety of races and religions, and would usually go to a place of a different race and religion from their own.

'The idea', Jim said, 'was to grow it to be something like the Peace Corps, but multinational, multi-ethnic, and concerned with the big problems of the twenty-first century. It was vitally important to try to spot future T-Generation leaders, and turn them into global citizens.'

To take off, the idea would need major funding from a big Foundation, like the Ford Foundation, in order to be able to send many hundreds of T-Generation students out per year. To make this happen, Tom and Jim decided to demonstrate the concept with Jim funding the first year. After some trial and error, ten young people from different countries and religions, aged from twelve to twenty-two, were signed up for what would be an adventurous year. They were all assigned to a country different from their own, given a brief training course at Merton College, Oxford while the university was on vacation, and then sent out 'into the field'. This was to be the proof of concept.

Jim decided to do a spot check and drop in unexpectedly on one of them at his field location.

'He was a fourteen-year-old Christian black boy from Uganda and we had sent him to Pune (pronounced 'Poona') in India – a town that has existed since AD 937 – where he worked in a Hindu school that had some Muslim students. It was very impressive to see how he was handling himself, and how he was learning how different religions can understand one another. The headmistress said he was a "godsend". We need to do much more to help young people to integrate between cultures.'

After a year, the ten young people came back to Merton College for a two-week debriefing. They all made presentations about their adventures, which were videotaped.

'They all seemed to have become different people,' Jim remembers. 'In different ways they had all become leaders. All of them said they didn't want to stop. They had amazing stories to tell. A consultant monitored the two weeks, and suggested that the World Education Corps change its name to "World Leadership Corps". We had achieved proof of concept spectacularly, but slowly realized that none of the big foundations would take the slightest interest in it.

'The very greatest wealth doesn't stem from capital, labour, minerals or land like it used to – it comes from the intellect. The mega-rich of an ideas economy are people like Bill Gates and Michel Dell and this changes the whole map of the world. Ideas, unlike most other resources, can come from anywhere, but they are more likely to come from an area with good universities. That is how India is starting to transform its terrible poverty.

'For the eventual balance to be right we need a whole generation of wise leaders, people who can see the broader vision of the future's possibilities. Progression towards any vision is always going to be blocked by catastrophes, bureaucrats, battles and distractions, but if we stay on course we can overcome all of them and steer the planet away from a course that would lead to mayhem and set the stage for an extraordinary evolution of civilizations very different from anything we know today.

'We have to ask: what is the right thing to do, rather than constantly worrying about what is the most likely thing to happen.'

The largest gatherings of computer people on the planet are usually the annual International Computer Conferences in Asia. They often have as many as ten thousand people attending.

Just such a conference was being held in Hong Kong in 2001. The theme was how information technology can change the world in the new century and Jim was the opening keynote speaker, giving a ninety-minute speech on Technology of the Future, starting at 9.30am on September 11th 2001.

The night before a Baha'i dinner had been arranged in a hotel overlooking the harbour so that attendees could hear Jim talk about the twenty-first century and then debate what he had said. There were two High Court judges present – one was a Chinese man and the other an English man. The

English judge was criticizing Jim for underestimating the resentment of America that was being experienced in some of the less-well-off countries. In the middle of the discussion the event organizer's husband rang her from New York saying that he had been just about to enter the World Trade Center building when a jumbo jet had hit one of the towers.

Fifteen minutes later the phone rang again to say the second tower had been hit. After that the phone circuits were totally blocked. The organizer tried to get a television or radio brought to the private suite where the dinner was being held, but everyone was too distracted. The group spent the rest of the evening with no phone, no radio and no television. It was like a bizarre evening at the theatre.

'The worst thing about this', the Chinese High Court judge said, 'is that it should happen while George Bush is President. Imagine how he will react.'

All four of Lillian's children were in Manhattan. All through the night she struggled to get through to New York while Jim re-wrote his lecture for 9.30 the following day. (There was a twelve-hour time difference.)

By the morning the whole speech had been changed to take in these dramatic events and at the end he asked for questions. Normally at a moment like that hands would shoot up all round the room, but this time he found himself looking at a sea of thousands of faces, their eyes averted.

'I'm not going to leave this stage until at least one of you has asked a question,' he said, and waited in silence.

A Chinese man timidly raised his hand. 'IBM has just introduced its first 64-bit z/OS operating system. This supports license manager technology. Is that significant?'

Jim stared at him, shocked. He attempted to answer, before trying again.

'The events of last night were so extraordinary,' he said, pausing for a moment. 'Are there any questions about the future?'

Another hand went up. 'Does the new Resource Director make z900 mainframes capable of shifting processor power across a network? Is it possible to automatically adapt to fluctuations in workloads?'

It was gradually dawning on Jim that he no longer wanted to concentrate on the minutiae of the technology industry. There were much bigger questions that needed answering than details about new models of computers. He wanted to spend all his time thinking about the future of humankind and the planet we inhabit. He wanted to write a book on the whole complex subject.

His next stop after Hong Kong was Kuala Lumpur, where he was due to give a talk on around the hundredth floor of one of their twin towers, which at that stage were the tallest buildings in the world. Since Malaysia is a Muslim country, many feared that the towers in Kuala Lumpur might be the first target for Western reprisals.

As Jim stood at a window watching a lightning storm, the alarms went off and everyone started shouting that the building had to be evacuated. They couldn't take the lifts and so had to begin the hundred-floor descent down the emergency stairwells with no idea what might happen to them next.

When they finally reached the bottom Jim began to wander around, looking for something to do to pass the time. He came across a magnificent concert hall in the basement of the tower where a famous Scandinavian conductor was giving a concert, apparently unconcerned about whatever might be happening in the world above.

As Jim sat listening to the beautiful music he remembered a scene he had written in Technology's Crucible *back in 1987, in which he had predicted an Arab terrorist attack on New York. His book had predicted the date as 1998 – three years out.*

He began to list the twenty-first century's biggest problems and opportunities. There was so much research to be done, so many things to learn. He was already approaching seventy, but he had no intention of retiring. Bertrand Russell's words were still with him and he truly believed that people who worked with their brains should never retire; that you can always continue learning as long as you are not struck down by dementia or any of the other debilitating illnesses.

Not wanting to be restricted by an editor, he set about writing the whole book without a publisher, a task that eventually took him five years. The book was The Meaning of the 21st Century.

CHAPTER EIGHTEEN
Refining the Human Body

Needing to check that my recording machine was working properly, I fumbled around in my pockets to find my glasses and noticed Jim watching me as I hunted.

'Don't you wear glasses at all then?' I enquired, suddenly realizing that I had never seen him with any, wondering if perhaps he used contact lenses but unable to imagine him being bothered with such fiddly accessories.

'I've got new eyeballs,' he grinned. 'About eighteen months ago my eyes were starting to play up and Lillian dragged me to an optician, who told me I would be blind in five years because I had fast-growing cataracts on my eye lenses. He sent me to a surgeon – a drop-dead-gorgeous lady in hotpants. She told me she would take my eyeballs out, clean them, fill them to inflate them and fit acrylic lenses, using a microprocessor to get them into exactly the right position. I just wanted to scream. It felt like I was taking part in a real-life horror film. She told me I had no serious choice. Three days after the operation she took the bandages off. It was a relief to see a glint of light, then to see objects, then the window.'

Once all the bandages had come off Jim thought something had gone horribly wrong. Everything he looked at was jittering around, but the doctor told him not to worry.

'Your brain has to deal with two objects it's never seen before,' she explained. 'Artificial eye lenses. The neurons in your brain have to re-learn how to process the new information your eyes are sending them. They have to learn what it means. They are busy re-connecting the wiring, forming new pathways. The brain has an amazing capability to rewire itself.'

'How long will this take?' Jim asked, imagining she might say three months.

'At your age, maybe half an hour.'

It was actually ten minutes before the jittering stopped and Jim's brain got the hang of the new lenses.

'I found I could read without glasses. I could see the leaves on distant trees. That night I could see every dot in the Milky Way.

'This is basically how we will be modifying ourselves in future. We are entering the era of regenerative medicine, regenerating old cells or worn-out body parts with the use of stem cells.'

I had already read Jim's explanation about stem cells in his book. When a human sperm first fertilizes an egg, a stem cell is formed that has the potential to transform into any type of cell in the human body. It then splits into two cells, then four, then eight and so on. About four days after fertilization a hollow sphere of cells forms that has an outer layer that will eventually form the placenta that is used to protect the development of the foetus while it becomes an embryo. These cells can be extracted and stored indefinitely at low temperatures and have the potential to develop into muscle cells, heart cells, brain cells, liver cells and about two hundred other types of mature cell. Other cells have been found to have this 'pluripotent' capability. They can then be multiplied in laboratory dishes and injected into a part of a body that has cell damage. There they can replace the damaged cells, then multiply and repair the tissue. This is one of the most important developments in medicine, ever.

'There are so many potential applications for regenerative medicine,' Jim enthused, 'particularly when it comes to rejuvenating an elderly person's immune system. It could start with the rejuvenation of eyes. People could end up being given cells at the age of seventy that are the same as the ones they were born with. In about twenty years' time it will be common practice, which will lead to a rapid evolution. Other technologies may well enable us to live until we are a hundred and twenty years old or more, and we don't want to be spending the last thirty or forty years of that span in wheelchairs because of our aging immune systems, and stem cells will be where the answers come from.'

The Oxford Stem Cell Institute, one of the Institutes of The 21st Century School, occupies the location where the first pioneering research on antibiotics was done at Oxford.

'At the same time scientists are making big strides in their understanding of the brain and its chemistry. Our ability to control the levels of serotonin, dopamine, epinephrine and other chemicals in the brain enables us to control our feelings of happiness, self-esteem, aggression, nervousness, depression, fear and wellbeing, as well as euphoric behaviour – all the things that we would describe as our "personalities". But better-targeted drugs are on their way, many of which will be tailored to the individual.'

Human brains could also be linked to technology and computer networks in the age of The Singularity, giving us the capability to be more or less 'on-line' in our heads in the same way our computers can be today.

'We will have a brain–computer interface with small metal plates attached to our skulls,' Jim explained, 'which will communicate by wireless to neurons. Nanotechnology devices the size of blood cells will clamp on to neurons, signalling to one another by wireless and also to things outside the brain. The brains will learn to use the new devices, just as mine learnt to use the new messages coming from my artificial eye lenses. Already a hundred thousand deaf people have cochlear implants connected directly to neurons in the brain – bionic ears. Eventually every human brain will have the potential to be connected into the network of computers that will straddle the earth, adding artificial functionality to the brain. This could start happening twenty years from now.'

'Brave New World,' I said. 'My god.'

'This and other technology will change the nature of being human. At the moment our brains send signals incredibly slowly, travelling at chemical speeds. Electronic signals can travel at the speed of light, maybe half a billion times faster than a human brain. You'll get intelligence improving itself at electronic speeds. But it will be a fundamentally different kind of intelligence. It won't just mean being able to do incredible mathematical calculations – we might also be able to build in a capability to better appreciate aesthetics, like music.

By this stage I had managed to find my glasses and was struggling to catch up with Jim's torrent of ideas.

'If we can connect the brain to the internet,' I mused, 'and we live to be a hundred and twenty or more, and most jobs can be done by machines, how will we spend our lives?'

'That's the interesting question. What worlds will we build?'

In 2008, before the financial meltdown, Jim was asked to go to a high-level conference in Moscow, near the Kremlin. The subject was what actions Russia should take to make its economy as strong as possible by 2020. It was bitterly cold. The Russians lent Jim a thick fur coat and a fur hat. At some conferences in Russia everyone dresses in shabby clothes, but in this one the delegates were in expensive suits with silk handkerchiefs spilling from their top pockets. There were large banners across the main street advertising Lamborghini cars with prices of up to $400,000.

Jim chaired a panel with four Russian ministers. He was told, 'Pull no punches. Tell them how America got rich.' So he talked about the giant American success stories: IBM, Google, Microsoft, Cisco, eBay and so on.

'My big message was for them to stop investing Russian money in American real estate and to invest it in their own scientists. Their mathematicians and physicists are brilliant: they should be investing in nanotechnology, stem cells, regenerative medicine, intelligent robotics, pre-Singularity computing, extreme-bandwidth networking and so on. They need to educate entrepreneurs, attract venture capitalists. I had a fight on my hands because the ministers were communists in sheep's clothing. But the silk-handkerchief crowd was all on my side.

'I was asked to film a TV show based on the BBC's *Hard Talk*. The thirty-minute programme took four hours to film, and there was heavy editing, so you had to be careful. There was elaborate make-up and the cameras raced around on circular tracks to finely adjusted spotlights. The interviewer, who was as smooth as Johnnie Walker Blue, said "I believe you enthuse about nanotechnology, stem cell medicine (the usual suspects). Prime Minister Putin would completely agree with you."

'"Good," I said. "He's right."

'"He's making big, big investments in them for Russia's future."

'"That's great."

'"He's going to own ten per cent of the investments personally …"

'"CUT!" I put my hand up. "That's not going out under my name!" The interviewer just smiled.'

When John Hood was about to take up the post of Vice Chancellor of Oxford in 2004, he came out to Gunpowder Island to talk with Jim about the big ideas of the twenty-first century. He knew that Jim wanted to be involved but he

wanted to ask what Oxford should be doing on a wider canvas, how it could be doing work that would make a difference in the world. Jim came up with a list of about twenty subjects that he felt the university should be concentrating on in general, subjects that we need to master in order to make a big difference. Thirteen of them were high priority.

'The transition from a planet on a self-destructive course', Jim told him, 'to a planet that is intelligently managed is the meaning of the twenty-first century. Even without the approaching changes in technology this would be vitally important, but technology is going to transform everything we do. It will unleash enormous quantities of human knowledge, represented in ways that computers can use.'

Their talks led to the idea of the school, and John also used them as a basis for raising over £1 billion in research grants in the coming years. Having now ended his time at Oxford he was due back on Gunpowder Island a couple days after we had gone, to talk some more.

The incoming Vice Chancellor and John Hood's replacement, Andrew Hamilton from Yale, also came to talk to Jim about the future.

'He knows the world will be changing in extraordinary ways during his seven years at the helm of Oxford,' Jim says. 'The rapid evolution of the internet has already caused turmoil in the music industry, and will do the same in the film industry. Most newspapers will go out of business. Television news networks will be made hopelessly obsolete and there will be turmoil in education. What should the role of a great university be when communities are worldwide and have extreme-bandwidth networking and electronic books?

'The world will need all the intellectual resources it can muster to deal with self-amplifying climate change, water running out and cheap weapons of mass destruction. Oxford

has remained on top throughout the mayhem of almost 900 years of English history – the civil wars, world wars, the black death, bishops being burnt at the stake, the break from the Vatican. How will it cope with The Singularity, transhumanism, economic meltdowns, fundamentalist Islam, hypersonic cruise missiles and the need for global governance of a planet that is cooking?

'The problem is that our wisdom is not accelerating at the same rate as science and technology. If these challenges can be handled with appropriate wisdom, they will put us in good shape for the centuries ahead. The next decade is critical in the long landscape of human history.

'The world must have global universities dealing with global interdisciplinary problems. It is significant that Andrew Hamilton is a scientist from a top American University. Oxford's tutorial system and college structure are beginning to work wonderfully with worldwide students.'

CHAPTER NINETEEN
The Greatest Crime Imaginable

Lillian kindly offered to drive us to the airport for our flight back to London and we loaded our cases on to the golf cart that had first brought them up to the house from the dock a week before.

'Lillian and Sue can drive to the dock', Jim said, 'and we'll walk down and meet them there.'

As the cart purred off on the circuitous route that avoided all the various steps and stairs, we made our way down the side of the quarry at the front of the house. Jim was talking fast, as if it was urgent now that he got what he had to say off his chest before it was too late and we had left the island.

'We have to find a way of making the world understand what is at stake here,' he said as we passed beneath the protective glare of the giant Chinese lions.

'Young people need to know that it isn't all gloom and doom. On the contrary – it's the most exciting time in history to *be* young. If humanity's young people make the right choices, collectively, they can have the most glorious future. We can build a civilization that is enormously better than the one we have today – a new *belle époque*.'

There were new flowers in the walls we passed. Even in the week that we had been on the island dozens of different species had burst into bloom along the side of the path to the dock and the sea reflected a shimmering sunlight on to their new petals.

'You know, the first creatures on earth to crawl out of the sea appeared about 660 million years ago. Suppose that a full-length feature film two hours long showed the progression of creatures from then until now. A second would represent 92,000 years of evolution. The whole of human civilization would be in just the last two or three frames of the film. The time from the first use of machines in the Industrial Revolution until the present day would be 0.004 seconds. It would be as if an almost instantaneous explosion had occurred.

'Homo sapiens is incredibly special – probably unique in the galaxy. There is nothing else like us and never has been. We are totally isolated and alone. But we are like small children. Imagine what Homo sapiens will be like when we grow up.

'Compared with the rest of evolution this is an extraordinary anomaly. Are humans today an outrageous aberration, or are we the beginnings of something utterly magnificent, like a parched desert bursting into bloom in springtime? Are super-intelligent creatures inevitable when a species achieves a certain level of complexity? Could something like this have happened in far-away parts of the universe? Do creatures evolve slowly for hundreds of millions of years and then suddenly learn to write, accumulate knowledge in machines, create universities and discover technology that is infinite in all directions?

'Evolution corrects its mistakes – the survival of the fittest. The capability for nuclear war may be just such a mistake. Will it be corrected by a cataclysm, or will we have the intelligence to correct it ourselves without a cataclysm?

'The fundamental question of our time is: will Homo sapiens survive? If it does survive, will it learn from its mistakes? If we understand this century and learn how to play its very complex game our future will be magnificent. If we get it wrong we may be at the start of a new type of Dark Age. Or worse, we may be extinguished.

'To extinguish something as extraordinary as Homo sapiens through carelessness would be the greatest crime imaginable. It would be the most terrible evil because we are on the cusp of evolving into something so incredible – a new Renaissance, millions of times beyond the Renaissance of Florence. It would be too tragic for words if we fail to get there and Homo sapiens is gone because of some madness in this century.

'Put this in your book. People need to understand that it is just the beginning. We must be absolutely determined that Homo sapiens will survive. We need to know what it will be like if we go through one more frame of the film. Humanity can act with utter determination when it has to. Young people need to understand they have a choice between creating a new Renaissance or a hell on earth. We need to understand the course we are on – not one course really, but thousands of courses. We need to give young people the strongest determination to get through this incredible century.'

'And how do we do that?'

'We need thousands of change agents to guide humanity through its biggest change ever.'

Lillian took the helm of the skiff to ferry us across and Jim stood waving on the dockside, beside a blazing display of yellow orchids. He wanted to get back to his tower in order to prepare his thoughts for John Hood's arrival in a few days.

'Can we just pop in and see Paul before we go to the airport?' Sue asked as we approached the mainland and Tucker danced out from behind the cottages to welcome us. 'I'd like to say goodbye.'

Paul helped us lift our cases up the steps. We loaded them into Lillian's car and followed him into his 'hobbit hole', ducking beneath pergolas and hanging baskets, squeezing past plants and driftwood sculptures, and were welcomed into the two small rooms that he and Tucker shared. Paul enthusiastically showed us his work and pictures of a grand garden he had once worked on in England, which looked like the sort of estate Jim and his childhood friends had trespassed on in Ashby-de-la-Zouche. When we finally had to go he presented Sue with something swathed in an aged plastic bag. Inside the bag, as Sue gently unwrapped it, was some recycled bubblewrap, which was protecting a small, lovingly varnished sculpture made from a delicate piece of Gunpowder Island driftwood.

'I thought it would be a more practical size for travelling than most of them,' he smiled nervously, glancing at some of the giant sculptures surrounding him.

This dainty piece of eco art, which had obviously been a pleasure for Paul to make and was now a pleasure for Sue to receive, was a poignant contrast to the mighty, empty-looking mansions and sleek white boats lying idle in the pretty little bays we drove past as Lillian delivered us back to the airport at the other end of Bermuda.

As Jim and I shook hands on the dock I asked him if he had any last words.

'Whatever will humanity be like in a hundred years' time?' he said. 'A thousand years? Ten thousand years? Will our progeny still be active in ten million years? The magnificence of what human civilizations will achieve if they continue for several centuries is utterly beyond anything we can possibly imagine.'

About the Author

Andrew Crofts has published more than eighty books over forty years as an author and ghostwriter, many of which have become international number-one bestsellers. His subject matters and co-authors have ranged from billionaires to bonded labourers, reality television stars to the rulers of medium-sized countries, rock stars to bar girls. He is also a travel writer, a business writer and a published novelist.